CARELESS TALK
COSTS LIVES

CARELESS TALK
COSTS LIVES

FOUGASSE AND THE ART OF
PUBLIC INFORMATION

JAMES TAYLOR

CONWAY

For Elizabeth and Rosemary Taylor

First published in 2010 by
Conway
An imprint of Anova Books Ltd
10 Southcombe Street
London W14 0RA
www.conwaypublishing.com
www.anovabooks.com

A CIP catalogue for this book is available from the British Library.

ISBN 9781844861293

Distributed in the U.S. and Canada by:
Sterling Publishing Co., Inc.
387 Park Avenue South
New York, NY 10016-8810

Printed and bound by Toppan Leefung Printing Limited, China

To receive regular email updates on forthcoming Conway titles,
email conway@anovabooks.com with Conway Update in the subject field.

CONTENTS

ACKNOWLEDGEMENTS

From an early age the author's mother made him conscious that during every phone conversation someone, other than the intended party, might be listening. Born and brought up in the shipbuilding city of Sunderland she has never forgotten the messages of the Home Front propaganda of World War II, notably the anti-gossip and rumour campaigns warning that 'Careless Talk Costs Lives'. It is thanks to her that Fougasse is the subject of this publication.

In addition many others deserve recognition and praise for their help, encouragement and support. They include the Bird family – Nicky Bird, Sarah Bird and Tom Bird; Dr Mark Bryant; Chris Beetles; Michael St John-McAlister, Curator, Department of Manuscripts, British Library; Anita O'Brien, Curator, The Cartoon Museum; staff of the Fine Arts Society; Richard Slocum, Jenny Wood, Jane Rosen and the staff of the Imperial War Museum; staff of King's College, London; David Langdon; Dr Bex Lewis; Frances Marshall and Sean Waterman, Museum of London; Nicholas Malton, Records Manager, NSPCC; Peter D. Dickinson, Miranda Taylor; Andre Gailani and Helen Walasek, *Punch* Magazine Archive and Library (past and present staff); staff of Austin Reed; Javier Molina and staff of Henry Sotheran Ltd; Robert Excell, London Transport Museum; the staff of the British Library, National Archives, Kew and Tate Britain; Dr James K. Kirkwood OBE, Chief Executive and Scientific Director Universities Federation for Animal Welfare; the staff of the Cartoon Art Centre, University of Kent; the Special Collections, University of Sussex; Catherine Flood and Christopher Marsden and the staff of the Victoria & Albert Museum; Berenice Webb, Webb Academy; and the generous contribution of Dr Paul Rennie; also Robert Dudley Literary Agency; John Lee and Alison Moss of Conway (Anova Books).

INTRODUCTION

Fougasse was one of the most popular cartoonists and illustrators of the first half of the twentieth century. Two of his collaborative publications *Aces Made Easy* (1934) and *You Have Been Warned: A Complete Guide to the Road* (1935), are still enjoyed today. The former illustrated the rules and etiquette of the game of contract bridge, and it ran into several editions. He is arguably the best-known and loved creator of British propaganda poster art. The images and captions to his series of eight World War II propaganda posters 'Careless Talk Costs Lives' are remembered fondly by the millions who experienced life on the Home Front, perhaps more so than 'Keep It Dark', 'Is Your Journey Necessary', 'Make-Do and Mend' and 'Dig For Victory'.

'Was he [Fougasse], some wondered, a Frenchman, imported because our cartoonists were not funny enough?'[1] In fact, he was an Englishman called Cyril Kenneth Bird who adopted the pseudonym because *Punch* already had a regular contributor who used the pen name Bird. His first cartoon appeared in 1916 when the magazine, then Britain's most popular and best-selling humorous weekly, published 'War's Brutalising Influence', and he signed with the name Fougasse; this being a type of crude French land mine which might, or might not, go off. He modestly thought the same of his cartoons. Fougasse would have a long, intimate and rewarding relationship with *Punch* magazine.

" Snap   What do you mean, Snap ? "

CHAPTER 1
FOUGASSE'S LIFE & CAREER

Fougasse was born on 17 December 1887 at 26 Westbourne Terrace Road, close to Paddington railway station in London. His grandfather, known as 'Iron' Bird, was a metal merchant who bought steel in South Wales and sold it in South America for their new railways. He lived close to Kenwood House in north London. He eloped and later married Sara Buck and had 10 children: Arthur, Fougasse's father, was one of the youngest.

Arthur Bird worked in the family-owned wine business Justerini & Brooks, of which his brother George was managing director. Arthur was a very good cricketer, a crack shot and an enthusiastic golfer. He died of a heart attack on Beaconsfield Golf Course. Fougasse went to Warwick House day school (1893–98) followed by Farnborough Park in Hampshire until 1902, and then obtained a scholarship to Cheltenham College (1902–04) where he excelled academically. He became head boy and maintained close links with the school. From 1954 to 1955 he was president of the Cheltonian Society.[1]

After leaving school he wanted to become an artist but his father put an end to his plans by telling him 'he would never be rich enough to keep him'. Instead he studied civil engineering at King's College in London (1904–08) where he was active as president of the University Union and the Engineering Society. He competed for King's in the boxing ring and on the rugby field. Fougasse also studied art, photography and lithography at evening classes at the Regent Street Polytechnic and the School of Photo Engraving in Bolt Court, now part of the University of the Arts, London. His many designs, cartoons and logos for

King's College literature, including menu cards for the King's Engineering Society, are available to view today in the College library.

Fougasse's studies at King's also coincided with his role for the Artists' Rifles (AR) working as a machine gun instructor. Raised in London in 1859 as a volunteer light infantry unit, the regiment saw active service during the Boer War and World War I, earning a number of battle honours. He was in good company: celebrated artists associated with the AR have included, Ford Maddox Brown, William Holman Hunt, John Everett Millais, Dante Gabriel Rossetti, Lord Leighton, the cartoonists and illustrators Charles Keene and John Leech, also John and Paul Nash. Alfred Leete (1882–1933) was also part of the regiment. Leete first contributed to *Punch* in 1905 but this British cartoonist is best known for the Lord Kitchener poster design which first appeared on the cover of the weekly magazine *London Opinion* in 1914. It was originally entitled 'Your Country Needs You'. It was adapted to encourage recruitment in Britain, America and elsewhere, and would have been a propaganda poster familiar to Fougasse. It was also adapted as an anti-gossip poster during World War II.

It would have come as no surprise to Fougasse that his extensive extra-curricula activities and sporting prowess had a detrimental effect on his primary studies and in 1908 he was awarded a Third Class BSc in Civil Engineering. However, this did not prevent him working initially as a civil engineer and becoming an Associate Member of the Institution of Civil Engineers on 28 February 1919.

After graduation he was sent to Spain by the Steel Company of Scotland to survey iron mines and in the following year he joined the company of civil engineers Easton, Gibb & Son at Rosyth, the Royal Navy dockyard near Edinburgh. He worked on various projects including submarines, and probably the three graving docks, where the hulls of ships were repaired and maintained, until he was called up for active war service.

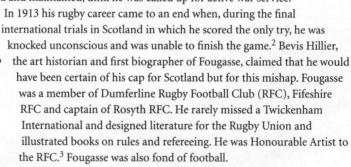

In 1913 his rugby career came to an end when, during the final international trials in Scotland in which he scored the only try, he was knocked unconscious and was unable to finish the game.[2] Bevis Hillier, the art historian and first biographer of Fougasse, claimed that he would have been certain of his cap for Scotland but for this mishap. Fougasse was a member of Dumferline Rugby Football Club (RFC), Fifeshire RFC and captain of Rosyth RFC. He rarely missed a Twickenham International and designed literature for the Rugby Union and illustrated books on rules and refereeing. He was Honourable Artist to the RFC.[3] Fougasse was also fond of football.

While working in Scotland he met his future wife, the artist Mary ('Mollie') Holden Caldwell who was staying with her aunt near the naval base. Mollie was captivated by his sportsman's bearing and acute brown eyes. The Caldwells were well to do. Mollie's father, William Hay Caldwell from Morar Lodge, Invernesshire, was an extraordinary man. A scientist and paper manufacturer, he was a Fellow of Gonville and Caius College, Cambridge. In 1883 he had been awarded a travelling scholarship by the Royal Society, which he used to travel to Australia to study the duck-billed platypus. He is credited as the first to prove conclusively that this mammal did indeed produce eggs.[4]

Family money provided Mollie with an annual allowance of £300 to buy 'nice clothes'. On 16 September 1914 she married Fougasse in a low-key service at St Matthew's Church, Bayswater. Sadly the clothing allowance stopped. Their honeymoon was at The French Horn, Sonning-on-Thames. Mollie had developed medical complications during their engagement and she had a hysterectomy, so they were not able to have children, nor did they adopt. But throughout his working life Fougasse was active in supporting a wide range of child and youth charities including Boy's Clubs, Girl Guides Association and the National Association for the Prevention of Cruelty to Children (NSPCC). From 1924 to 1932 he was a Member of the Central Council of the NSPCC.[5]

On the outbreak of World War I in 1914 Fougasse joined the Army as a second lieutenant in the Special Reserves of the 52nd Division of Royal Engineers. He was not on active duty for long when, fighting at Gallipoli in 1915, a shell shattered his back and he was invalided home.

His original Invalidation Certificate, now in the Victoria & Albert Museum archives, is actually dated 16 April 1918. It shows an elaborate printed image with two soldiers standing before the seated figure of Britannia. Originally drawn in pen and ink by the senior *Punch* artist Bernard Partridge (1861–1945) the certificate states that he served with honour.

Bedridden and unable to walk Fougasse was literally flat on his back for three years. He recuperated first in the hospital in Vincent Square, Pimlico, and then moved with Mollie to a flat in Chelsea. During this time he had turned to cartooning as a form of distraction and entertainment. With a modest military pension and no prospect of returning to his pre-war career of civil engineering he initially considered writing short stories but rejection slips led him to focus

ACES MADE EASY

" I think he's coming round now, Doctor—he's just gone one no trump ! "

In 60 years,
the
NSPCC
has come to the rescue of
5½ MILLION CHILDREN

PLEASE HELP US, IF YOU CAN

THE NATIONAL SOCIETY FOR THE PREVENTION OF CRUELTY TO CHILDREN (DIAMOND
JUBILEE YEAR APPEAL), VICTORY HOUSE, LEICESTER SQUARE, LONDON, W.C.2.

on an artistic career, although he used his literary skills to brilliant and memorable effect in captioning his cartoons. Fougasse was an intellectual artist who wrote several books including a history of visual humour entitled *The Good-Tempered Pencil* (1956).

Determined to improve his technique he continued his art studies by correspondence through Percy Bradshaw's Press Art School. He had a gift to capture the illusion of movement in his cartoons. His early work though was typical of the late Victorian and Edwardian representational school – rather stiff and laboured with extensive cross-hatching. He gradually refined his technique and simplified his cartooning style reducing it to spare lines. It was innovative, unique and hugely popular. It was fully developed in the 1930s, and highly effective in conveying his chosen message. It drew people in to study his work more closely.[6] During the 1920s Fougasse first began to create designs for the London Underground, as well as doing humorous advertisements for Abdullah cigarettes. In the following decades he worked for Austin Reed, among many others companies.

When World War II broke out in 1939 Fougasse and Mollie worked as Air Raid Wardens and he offered his artistic services to the government free of charge. He worked for many of the Ministries and provided a wide range of design work for the Army, Royal Navy and Royal Air Force. He had strong views about propaganda posters that were articulated in his publication *A School of Purposes* (1946). He asserted that humour was more effective than horror for the messages in posters to be remembered and acted upon. His distinctive style of sharp linear images and gentle humour produced effective propaganda and information material. Fougasse's celebrated series of posters for the 'Careless Talk Costs Lives' campaign (1940) was devised to counter gossip and rumour that could be detrimental to the war effort.

Fougasse's designs encouraged the country to be more efficient and productive, to save energy, paper and time. One of his fuel economy labels depicts Hitler and Emperor Hirohito jumping up and down with joy captioned, 'Switched-on switches & turned-on taps, Make happy Huns & joyful Japs'. He also created humorous designs to prevent

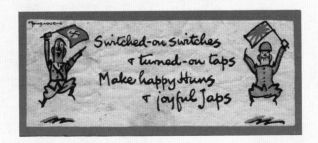

accidents at home and in the workplace, notably for the Royal Society for the Prevention of Accidents (RoSPA), to combat antisocial behaviour and noise in hospitals with tag-lines such as 'Clatter Does Matter' and 'Noise Seldom Adds to Our Joys' (printed for King Edward's Hospital Fund), as well as posters and pamphlets highlighting the futility of gambling, extolling the virtues of listening to live music at the Royal Albert Hall, enjoying national and provincial theatrical productions, and buying and reading books.

In the mid 1940s London Underground commissioned Fougasse to produce his finest transport posters reminding passengers, through his familiar 'formulaic' cartoon designs, of the rules, regulations and etiquette of public transport. The posters and a selection of original artwork can be seen in the London Transport Museum.

During his lifetime Fougasse's work was familiar the length and breadth of Britain and abroad too through his cartoons for *Punch* magazine – of which he became the editor in 1949 – posters and prolific book illustrations of diverse subjects that include the card game bridge, golf, road safety and rugby. He provided numerous artworks for technical and instruction manuals, wall charts for classrooms as an aid to learning French, as well as health and fitness posters. The themes of his work are topical today and connect with the challenges that face all developed nations, not least the issue of freedom of speech.

He was a remarkably generous supporter of a wide range of charities, donating artwork

The nuisance value of sound often bears little relation to its intensity.
(Report on Noise Control in Hospitals, King Edward's Hospital Fund for London)

NOISE
ALMOST ALWAYS ANNOYS

Published by King Edward's Hospital Fund for London from a drawing kindly presented by FOUGASSE   No.5   F. & C. Ltd.

and cartoons to leading and lesser known organisations including the Boys Clubs, the British and American Red Cross, the NSPCC, and the Universities Federation for Animal Welfare (UFAW). Founded in 1926, he had a particular fondness for this charity and his logo design for the organisation is still used today. It is estimated that his charitable work has helped to raise millions of pounds.

A genial, mild and modest man, in 1946 Fougasse was awarded a CBE (Commander of the Order of the British Empire) for his wartime services to the country, but for his services to charity alone he deserved to be knighted.

THE KILLJOY.

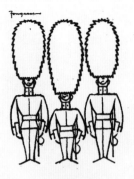

Height standard

CHAPTER 2

ARTISTIC TECHNIQUE, ADVERTISING & PUNCH MAGAZINE

From an early age Fougasse had a passion for drawing and displayed a nascent talent. Visitors to Mollie Bird's home at Forres in Inverness, where she retired after her spouse's death, were amazed that a small-scale watercolour of red roofs that he had painted at the age of 7 was not the work of an adult.[1]

In the Christmas of 1900 Fougasse received a present from his father of a sketch-book bound in green and maroon leather in which he drew several ink cartoons notable for their economic use of squiggly lines. In this book, and others, he started to develop images and jokes. He experimented with representational formats and comic devices that would later be worked up into the familiar fully fledged cartoons. These early efforts would pave the way for his mainstream subjects, themes and styles.

The Christmas sketch-book covers various subjects including scenes and topical jokes relating to the Boer War (1899–1902), fought between the British and the descendants of the Dutch settlers (Boers) in Africa. For example, 'Question: Why are our soldiers in S. Africa never dry? Answer: Because of The Wet (DeWet)'. Christiaan de Wet was a renowned Boer general, rebel leader and politician.

The sketch-book also featured some of his early rugby jokes, one of which, 'Backs and Half Backs', Hillier described as a 'Phil May-like' drawing. May (1864–1903) was an influential English cartoonist and contributor to *Punch*. This early attempt developed into

PORTRAIT OF A GENTLEMAN IN PROCESS OF DECIDING THAT THE HIRE OF A CAR TO TAKE HIM TO HIS FANCY-DRESS REVEL WOULD HAVE BEEN WELL WORTH THE EXPENSE.

more sophisticated coloured cartoons, such as 'All the same, you know, those aeroplanes that fly over Twickenham must get rather a jolly view of the game' (1932), where the humour hinges on what the players wear, how they appear at ground level and from an aerial viewpoint (see page 87). There was also an image of a 'Linesman' cleverly depicted in straight lines that also anticipates his mature work.

Humorists invariably have several techniques for making people laugh. In addition to his stand-alone cartoons Fougasse employed three main comic devices, or formats. The first was 'The Odd Man Out', evident in 'Portrait of a Gentleman in Process of Deciding…', where we can share the embarrassment of the man waiting on a platform for a train wearing fancy-dress much to the amusement of a large crowd clad in normal attire.

The second format, 'Before and After', was long-running and was perhaps best expressed in the popular series entitled 'The Changing Face of Britain', which contrasted everyday British life – the attitudes, experiences and situations of people prior to and during World War II.

By far the most popular format practised by Fougasse (and notably H. M. Bateman), up to the 1930s was the 'Episodic'[2]. Here Fougasse would create a series of scenes on one sheet that varied in number, but were normally eight, nine or twelve, sometimes more. These are usually read from top left to bottom right. In these episodic cartoons Fougasse favoured

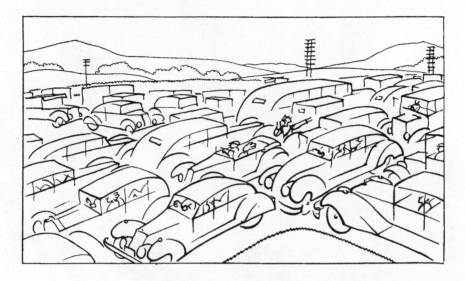

Hey for the Open Road—I

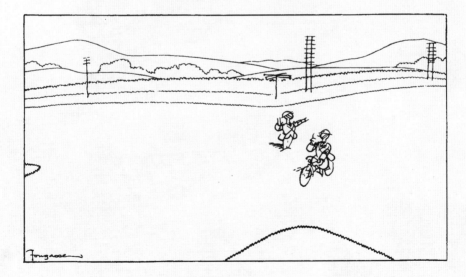

Hey for the Open Road—II

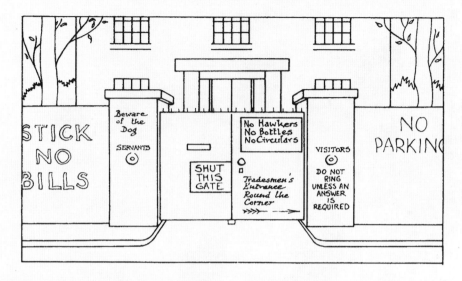

Englishman's House—I

Englishman's House—II

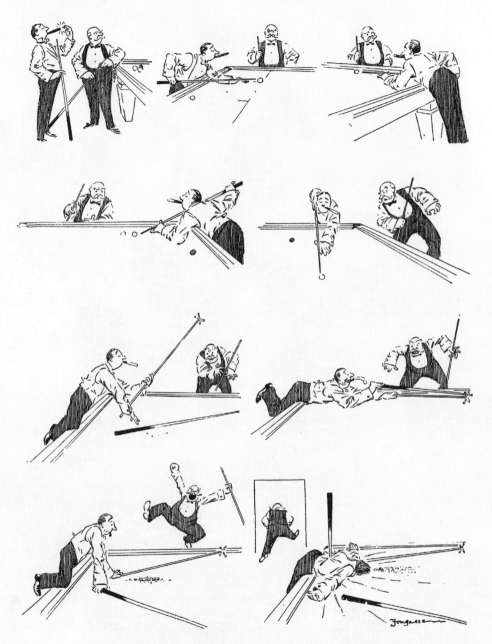

TRAGEDY OF A CIGAR-ASH.

Busman's holiday.

the approach of a cumulative joke, often leading up to an explosive climax or dramatic let down. Excellent examples include, 'Tragedy of a Cigar-Ash' and 'The Man Who Sneezed'. In the first of these Fougasse portrays two gentlemen playing snooker. One is smoking a cigar whilst playing. After each frame his opponent's expression gradually turns from disdain to growing frustration, anger and then finally leads to violence when the cigar ash falls onto the snooker table. An early example of this device is also evident in Fougasse's Christmas sketch-book. The format continued till the end of his working career, although it featured less.

One of the preliminary drawings for 'The Man Who Sneezed' (originally published in the *Punch* Almanack, 1 January 1921) has come to light, courtesy of Chris Beetles, a specialist dealer in illustrations and cartoons. They are pen-and-ink and pencil sketches on one sheet measuring 10½ x 7 inches. Considerably cruder in execution and overall design to the published image, it is perhaps his first attempt (see overleaf). Compared to the published picture it reveals some significant changes, especially in the third and fourth scenes. In the third of the published image the violinist is seen jumping in the air, although he is shown with his feet on the ground in the drawing. In the fourth scene of the drawing the violinist fixes a violent expression towards the sneezer, as opposed to the disdainful appearance apparent in the published image.

It is believed that Fougasse destroyed most of his preparatory work and so this makes it difficult to obtain a clear, coherent and accurate idea of his working approach. However, from this example we can discern that picture ideas were worked up until he was satisfied. Perhaps in-house *Punch* artists/designers and print-makers also helped to strengthen the lines, and hone, polish and re-calibrate his compositions. After all Fougasse was essentially a self-taught artist. Perhaps his wife provides the answer: 'He never made messes. He was wonderfully neat in everything he did. But he didn't draw the final cartoon straight off. He did dozens of sketches until he'd got it right'. Fougasse tried to seamlessly merge the joke with the cartoon. He admitted to one interviewer that he 'used the rubber more than the pencil'. The lengthy process of working up a final design was not unique to Fougasse. Abram Games OBE (1914–1996), a contemporary poster designer, would render up to 30 small preliminary sketches and then combine two or three into the final one.[3]

The French artist Caran d'Ache (1858–1909), the pseudonym of Emmanuel Poire, is oft cited as a dominant influence on Fougasse's 'Episodic' work. Born in Moscow, he emigrated to France where he worked as a satirist and political cartoonist. He is widely acknowledged as one of the precursors of the comic strips. However, there was another native practitioner who was almost certainly of greater influence; a man who used the moniker Dumb-Crambo Jr. Dumb Crambo was an old rhyming game. His real name was Joseph Priestman Atkinson (*c.*1840–1923) and he was a widely admired *Punch* cartoonist in the 1870s and 1880s.[4]

The source for suggesting the influence of Dumb-Crambo Jr on Fougasse derives from a paragraph in *The Star* newspaper of 27 January 1923:

> Mr. Joseph Priestman Atkinson, who has just died at home in Crescent Grove, that old-world backwater which faces the south side of Clapham Common, was the last surviving member of the staff of 'Punch' when Mark Lemon edited it. Mr. Atkinson's most notable contribution to 'Punch' was the 'Dumb Crambo' series of thumbnail sketches. They introduced the idea of a continuous story told in small sketches which Mr. Bateman [Henry Mayo Bateman] and Fougasse are popularising in 'Punch' now.

In 1912 Fougasse created 'The Life Class' in watercolour and ink that portrayed two artists painting a winged cherub precariously perched on a pedestal. The scene is almost certainly mocking the formal art schools, notably the Royal Academy of Arts (established in 1768) that in fact did not initially teach painting but rather drawing from antique models, sculptures and plaster models before the students graduated to draw directly from life models. Towards the end of the Edwardian era he created a charming pen-and-ink and coloured design he titled 'Stained Glass Window Designed While Waiting for the

Running away to sea.

The Man Who Sneezed

THE MAN WHO SNEEZED.

CRICKET CAN NEVER BE DULL.

WELL, ANYWAY, I DON'T SEE HOW CRICKET CAN EVER BE DULL TO THE PLAYER. I GRANT YOU THAT OUT OF EVERY TEN HOURS OF PLAY YOU SPEND ON AN AVERAGE (CORRECT ME IF I'M WRONG)—

Fougasse

TWO HOURS AND FIFTY MINUTES ON LUNCHEON AND TEA INTERVALS AND SUCH—

THREE HOURS WAITING IN THE PAVILION, DOING NOTHING—

AND TWENTY MINUTES WAITING AT THE BOWLER'S END AND BETWEEN OVERS, DOING VERY LITTLE—

ALSO TWO-AND-A-QUARTER HOURS WAITING IN THE FIELD, JUST WAIT-ING—

AND, IF IT COMES TO THAT, FIFTY MINUTES CROSSING OVER BETWEEN THE OVERS—

BUT, ALL THE SAME, YOU ARE ACTUALLY BATTING ON AN AVERAGE FOR FIFTEEN MINUTES, AND PERHAPS ACTUALLY MAKING SCORING STROKES FOR A WHOLE MINUTE-AND-A-HALF—

YOU ARE ACTUALLY IN PROCESS OF FIELDING A BALL FOR NO FEWER THAN FOURTEEN MINUTES—

YOU ARE ACTUALLY ON TO BOWL FOR NO FEWER THAN SIXTEEN MINUTES—

AND, POSSIBLY, FOR A GLORIOUS SEVEN SECONDS YOU'RE ACTUALLY TAKING A WICKET!

NOW SUPPOSE YOU PLAY SOME SILLY SOFT-BALL GAME LIKE TENNIS FOR TEN HOURS INSTEAD.

WELL, THE THING'S RIDICULOUS, BECAUSE—

YOU CAN'T POSSIBLY GO ON PLAYING TENNIS FOR TEN SOLID HOURS!

Postman'(1913), portraying 'Mr Postie' in a comic angelic pose with post bags and a red pillar box positioned behind.

By his own admission Fougasse was not a top-flight artist or draughtsman, but he had a talent for conveying speed, dynamism and movement with just a few stokes of his pen.[5] He was adept at depicting the sensation of speed of cars, planes and trains, and creating the illusion of the rapid movement of sportsmen, including a tennis player running around a court in such works as 'Mine, Partner'(circa 1920). His first publication *A Gallery of Games* (1921) was reviewed in the *Manchester Guardian* on 2 May 1922. The reviewer remarked that 'It is an interesting proof of the superiority of the artist over the machine that the figures of these sportsmen, as drawn by "Fougasse", are moving more rapidly over the printed page than any creatures of the kinema [Cinema]'.

Fougasse, however, was conscious that he needed further artistic tuition to improve his draughtsmanship. He opted for the popular correspondence course in illustration from the Press Art School, whose Headquarters were located at Tudor Hall, Forest Hill, situated in south-east London (SE23). This was set-up by Percy V. Bradshaw in 1905. He regularly advertised the school's services in *Punch*.

Percy Venner Bradshaw (1877–1965) was an artist, writer, illustrator, teacher and businessman. He was the principal of the Press Art School for 50 years. He recommended drawing as an ideal low-cost self-improvement hobby that would remain fun and interesting all year round.

Bradshaw further claimed in an advertisement in *Punch*, 17 February 1926, that: 'I have

" MINE, PARTNER."

taught drawing to thousands of people since 1905…Many of the leading illustrators of today are my old pupils. Upwards of a thousand sketches by old pupils have appeared in *Punch* alone.'[6]

There is little doubt that Fougasse found the artistic tuition beneficial, although one fundamental aspect of his own work certainly could not be taught by correspondence, as it is arguably largely innate. It is a sense of humour. Fougasse's 'delightful sense of nonsense' shines through in his advertisements, artwork, cartoons, designs, illustrations and posters.

Fougasse was born in the late Victorian age before the dawn of motion pictures and colour photography. As full-colour print reproduction was in its infancy and hugely expensive for a large part of Fougasse's working life he worked within a black-and-white world enlivened with tonal highlights, cross-hatching (in his early work) and shading. His first efforts aped the established senior hands of *Punch*. He had as a boy been an avid reader of *Punch* magazine. His personal collection of magazines can now be seen in the V&A Fougasse Archive.

Across his career Fougasse worked for various newspapers and numerous illustrated weeklies and monthlies, such as *Aeroplane, Animal Lovers Annual, Blighty, Bystander* (22 illustrations), *Children's Newspaper, Country Life, Evening News, Fun Fair, Gaiety, Graphic, Haagsche Post Illustrated* (Holland), *Land & Water* (5 illustrations), *Life* (USA) (6 illustrations), *Listener, London Magazine, London Opinion* (54 illustrations), *Nash's Illustrated Weekly, New Yorker* (USA), *London Magazine, Out & Away, Pan* (3 illustrations), *Pears Annual* (5 illustrations), *Pearson's Magazine* (7 illustrations), *Pearson's Weekly, Radio Times* (2 illustrations), *Royal Magazine* (5 illustrations), *Sketch* (62 illustrations), *Sporting and Dramatic News, Sportsman, Star, Strand* magazine (5 illustrations), *Tatler* (12 illustrations), *Tit-Bits, Welcome* and *Woman's Home Companion* (USA).[7]

But the one magazine that he was most closely associated with was *Punch*. In Fougasse's personal work record book he provided details of all his paid and unpaid work. He noted that his *Punch* contributions ranged from 19 July 1916 to 31 December 1963 and the number of cartoons published was 1,846.

His first drawing to be signed Fougasse –'War's Brutalising Influence' – was published in *Punch* on 19 July 1916. One image shows a young dandified officer perfectly attired in his pristine military uniform. His narrow waist and rounded feminine face make a stark contrast with his companion portrait of an angular-jawed officer whose uniform has clearly seen military action. The 'dandy' smokes a cigarette, perhaps a small cigar, and is portrayed as a 'cardboard cut out'. As Hillier observed, he resembles an image 'straight out of a military outfitter's catalogue'. There is no depth or substance to this effete individual compared to the gritty realism of war personified by the pipe-smoking figure, who is realistically rendered through convincing perspective, posture and dramatic *chiaroscuro* and shadows. He is the 'real soldier', although the dark colouring, his wild staring eye and

"GADGETS."

WAR'S BRUTALISING INFLUENCE.

Fashion Plate—Old Style.   Fashion Plate—New Style.

grim expression reveal he has been deeply affected by war.

It was accepted for publication by the acclaimed draughtsman Frederick Henry Townsend (1868–1920) who in 1905 became the first art editor of *Punch*, a position that Fougasse himself would hold in 1937. After Townsend's death he was also encouraged by another of the magazine's stalwarts, Frank Reynolds (1876–1953), who succeeded Townsend as art editor.

Punch, the magazine of humour and satire, ran from 1841 until its closure in 2002, although Miranda Taylor, a former *Punch* employee, notes that 'there was a bit of a hiatus when *Punch* closed in April 1992 (under United Newspapers Ltd). The Library and Archive remained at Ludgate House and was eventually purchased by Al Fayed in January 1996 and the first issue of the new *Punch* appeared in Sept 1996'. Its founders, the wood-engraver Ebenezer Landells and writer Henry Mayhew, got the idea from a French satirical paper, *Charivari* (the first issue was subtitled, 'The London Charivari'). The name *Punch* derived from an early meeting when someone remarked that the magazine should be like a good Punch mixture – nothing without Lemon; the magazine's founding editor was Mark Lemon (1809–1870).[8]

Punch was '…a very British institution with an international reputation for its witty and irreverent take on the world. It has published the work of some of the greatest comic writers including William Makepeace Thackeray, P. G. Wodehouse and P. J. O'Rourke among many others, and gave us the cartoon as we know it today. Its political cartoons swayed governments while its social cartoons captured life in the 19th and 20th centuries'.[9]

The world's finest cartoonists appeared there including John Tenniel, acclaimed as the first illustrator of *Alice in Wonderland* (1865) and E. H. Shepard, illustrator of *Winnie the Pooh* (1926). Fougasse was a neighbour and close friend of A. A. Milne (1882–1956), the creator of Eeyore, Kanga and Roo, Owl, Piglet, Rabbit, Tigger and Pooh bear. Mollie Bird recalled that on the night Christopher Robin was born, Milne wrote her a four-page letter about the event.[10] Milne wrote articles for *Punch*. Fougasse collaborated with him and Milne wrote a witty introduction to Fougasse's second publication *Drawn at a Venture* (1922) in which he noted that his cartoons 'make the very jokes which we should have made for ourselves, if only we had realised that they were jokes'.

It was within the pages of *Punch* that Fougasse would discover his own singular and instantly recognisable means of expression. He gradually pared down realistic figures into those comparable to a stylised linear rag doll. This process started in the late 1920s but was only fully realised in the 1930s. Some of the features of his figures are reminiscent of Jim Henson's popular puppet creations *The Muppets*. Perhaps Fougasse inspired Henson? Fougasse's realistic and rag doll drawings often featured within the same magazine. This is evident in the 'Festival of Britain' edition of *Punch* of 30 April 1951 in which the suggested humans of 'Mass Observation I & II' (see detail below) have the appearance of alien lifeforms, that dramatically contrast with the realistic and more traditional rendering of the figures in 'Our Predecessors' Games' (see page 88).

During the 1930s Fougasse continued his stylistic reduction process so that his subjects consisted of just a few simple elemental lines to suggest human form, expression and action. A close examination often reveals the absence of basic human features such as ears, eyes, nose and mouth. Hands and feet are often one or two hooks or sharp prongs, and yet he brilliantly manipulates his lines, creating the illusion of posture, gesture, expression and emotion. The viewer fills in, unwittingly, the bits that are missing.

The best-selling large annual almanacks published by *Punch*, which had bolstered the fortunes of the flagging magazine during its infancy also contributed to the fame and relative fortune of Fougasse. The success of these and also the collections of his cartoons in book format were so great that by the mid-1920s, he was well on the way to becoming a household name. This is borne out by a special commission to design a miniature book for Queen Mary's Doll's House. A. A. Milne and the prominent English essayist, parodist and caricaturist Max Beerbohm also contributed. The Doll's House was

completed in 1924 to a design by the architect Sir Edwin Luytens. Built to a scale of one inch to a foot it stands over three feet tall. It was created as a gift to Queen Mary from the people, and to serve as a historical document on how a royal family might live during that period in Britain. It was used to raise funds for the Queen's charities. Originally exhibited at the British Empire Exhibition 1924 and 1925, it is now on display in Windsor Castle.

Fougasse also received recognition through awards. In 1922 he became an Honorary Fellow of King's College, London. In 1924 and 1925 he was awarded the British Empire Exhibition Diploma, issued in appreciation of Services rendered in contributing to the representation of the Arts, Science and Industry of The British Empire. In 1937 he would receive a French award, the *Diplôme Commémoratif*, from the Exposition International Des Arts et Des Techniques, Paris.[11]

By the early 1920s Fougasse had been benefiting from representation by the artists' agents A. E. Johnson, based in Lincoln Chambers, 3 Portsmouth Street, London WC2. One of their promotional brochures has a delightful episodic cartoon cover by Fougasse's chief rival H. M. Bateman (1887–1970). He was also the creator of the wartime propaganda posters for the campaigns that carried the slogans 'Coughs and Sneezes Spread Diseases' and 'Don't Be Fuel-ish'. Bateman's cover is captioned 'An Episode in the Life of an Artists' Agent'.

After Fougasse's death Mollie adamantly maintained that it was her spouse, not Bateman, who created the first in the hugely popular series 'The Man Who…'. This series, according to Bateman's biographer, Anthony Anderson, featured '…comically exaggerated reactions to minor and usually upper-class social gaffes'. There may be some doubt about that assertion but it is now widely accepted that 'alongside H. M. Bateman he developed the strip cartoon in *Punch* and in advertisements'.[12]

A. E. Johnson represented commercial illustrators, cartoonists and fine artists. The brochure that survives in the London Transport Museum archives shows that Fougasse was in distinguished company. The roll-call of names reveals that in addition to Bateman, Bruce Bairnsfather (1888–1959), popularly known for his humorous series for the *Bystander* about life in the trenches, featuring 'Old Bill' (he also produced an anti-gossip poster in 1939), the *Punch* contributors Frank Reynolds, Ernest Shepard, W. A. Sillince and Norman Thelwell; the marine painter Frank Henry Mason (who produced the earliest pictorial propaganda poster of World War II);[13] sporting artist Lionel Edwards and the eminent landscape painter Edward Seago were on the books.

In 1925 Fougasse was commissioned by the London and North Eastern Railway (LNER) to design a poster. The LNER was the second largest of the 'Big Four' railway companies created by the Railways Act 1921. It was noticed by *The Daily Telegraph* on 26 May 1925: 'Fougasse has succeeded in executing that rare thing, a humorous poster, although the eccentric figure stretching out a carriage window to breathe the early-

THE REAL TRAFFIC PROBLEM.

WHAT DO YOU DO WHEN STORM'S PORT SAYS "STOP," BUT SPOT'S PILLS SAY "GO"?

morning air of Scotland, is transgressing all the company's by-laws'. Perhaps that is why he was not encouraged to produce further poster work for the railways. Fougasse recorded only one poster for LNER in his personal work book, and also just one for Imperial Airways, a precursor of British Airways. The latter, published circa 1930, portrays a winged waiter balancing a tray flying across the sky with the strap-line 'Travel comfortably…Europe, Africa, India, China, Australia'. After the Road Traffic Act of 1930 all British driving licences were standardised, and Fougasse was commissioned to create a small-scale brochure (designed to accompany the license) with humorous illustrations reminding drivers of the rules and regulations of the road.

Mollie was also enjoying artistic success. She was an accomplished painter in watercolours, mainly of views of the west coast of Scotland. She exhibited and sold her pictures in Glasgow, at the Royal Academy of Arts and the Fine Art Society, New Bond Street in London, sometimes jointly with her spouse. The press dubbed them Fougasse and Fougassine. They divided their time between Morar in Invernesshire for six months of the year, three months in London, and three in the South of France.[14]

In 1937 Fougasse succeeded George Morrow (1869-1955) as *Punch*'s art editor. Now contributors were encouraged to visit the office to discuss their work. He collaborated with Edmund Valpy Knox (1881–1971), the poet and satirist who wrote under the pseudonym Evoe, who was editor of *Punch* 1932–49, having been a regular contributor in verse and prose for many years, in modernizing the magazine's format, the layout and content, shortened captions to 'speed-up' the jokes and introduced two double-pages a week of descriptive reporting from around Britain.[15] According to Peter Mellini, who wrote the *Dictionary of National Biography* (*DNB*) entry for Fougasse, they '...injected a strong American advertising influence. His ideal was a cartoon that did not need a caption. A skilful humorist, he gently teased the English with his terse one-line captions. These reflected his awareness of a shortening in the audience's attention span, which resulted from the talking film and radio broadcasting.

It was not his preferred area of work but Fougasse produced some excellent humorous press and commercial advertisements. Given the choice of the relative freedom and independence of working for *Punch* or the critical judgement and constraints of companies and corporations not necessarily attuned to his work, it was clear that he favoured the former. However, his advertising work was another string to his artistic bow. He promoted a mind-boggling range of goods, products and services, including bacon, cameras, cigarettes, chocolates, custard powder, electricity, fireworks, insurance, peas, petrol, air and rail travel, soup, tea, tobacco, toffee, vacuum cleaners and whisky.

Fougasse was commissioned to produce work for the Automobile Association, Abdullah cigarettes, Australian Shipping Line, Blue Bird Laundry, Bushells Tea, Cadburys, EDA Electricity, C&A, Duff Gordon sherry, Gillette Razor Company, Harrison Steamship Line, Lapham Teas, Lever Bros, Manchester Ship Canal, Pearl Assurance, Pyramid Handkerchiefs, Richard Ogden jewellers, Southern Railway Holidays, Shell-Mex, Slumberland mattresses, Tootals and Yorkshire Relish.[16]

Fougasse had a brilliant gift for giving human

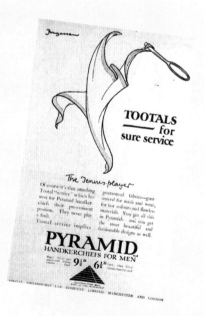

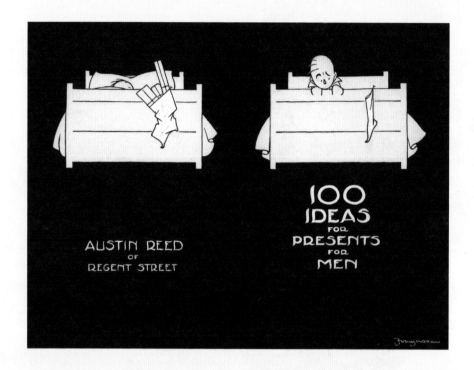

form and expression to inanimate objects. One of his creations for Pyramid handkerchiefs (Tootals) is entitled 'The Tennis Player'. The 'hanky' holds a tennis racket and is about to serve. The advert is cleverly captioned 'Tootals – for sure service'. Fougasse's work book reveals that he produced 27 posters for Tootals, the largest number for any company or organisation.

Perhaps his most successful and beneficial commercial relationship was with Austin Reed. In 1900 the company opened its first men's tailoring store in Fenchurch Street, London, and just over a decade later the flagship store in Regent Street was established. By the mid 1920s there were 12 stores across Britain. Working for them between the Wars, Fougasse's unique contribution in style and humour played a significant part in the success of the national advertising campaigns and helped to transform the publicity for menswear. Some of the original artwork has survived including: '100 Ideas for Presents for Men' drawn for Austin Reed's Christmas Book, November 1932, and 'Start your Holidays at Austin Reed', drawn for an Austin Reed Holiday poster and card, June 1933.[17] Fougasse's work book indicates that he designed 5 books, 10 posters and a staggering 227 press adverts for Austin Reed.

Fougasse designed the souvenir guide edition for the Royal Mail ship *Queen Mary* in 1936, the same year as her maiden voyage from Southampton to New York. The guide was published by Austin Reed, which had two shops on board. This celebrated Cunarder, an Art Deco floating wonder, is now a conference centre and hotel in Long Beach, California. Ocean liners were popular subjects for cartoonists. These vessels (in addition to airplanes) would carry Fougasse's cartoons and wartime posters to the USA, and prominent parts of the British Empire, notably Australia and Canada.

THIS REALLY
DOES
NEED YOUR SUPPORT

KENSINGTON WARSHIP WEEK
March 21 - 28

CHAPTER 3

WORLD WAR II 'CARELESS TALK COSTS LIVES'

Whan World War II broke out in 1939 Fougasse worked as an Air Raid Warden, and in keeping with his generous nature and patriotic personality he offered his artistic services to the government free of charge. He was offered a fee but declined it, stating that it was 'his contribution to the war effort'. Other artists were paid for their services and they included Dame Laura Knight (1877–1970), the English Impressionist painter well known for capturing the world of London's theatre, ballet and circus, also country and rural scenes. A letter in the British National Archives, dated October 21 1939, reveals that she was offered 10 guineas for a 'preliminary sketch' and a further 60 guineas for the finished design, to be 'processed only if the design was passed'.[1] Some of her work was declined. Among other work Knight produced designs for the 'Lend a Hand on the Land' campaign.

Fougasse dealt directly with the General Production Division (GPD), the technical division that produced the posters and other illustrational material under the Art Director and Studio Manager Edwin Joseph Embleton. His department was part of the Ministry of Information (MOI). Originally established towards the end of World War I, it was quickly reformed at the outbreak of World War II, as it was believed that this time round it would be a war of nerves. The HQ of the MOI was located in Senate House at the University of London, and acted as the central government department for publicity and propaganda. In 1940 there was a staff 1,000 strong.[2] George Orwell worked for the MOI, and this building

Have you any books
that would help to fill this?

If so, please send a p.c. to

ROYAL NAVAL WAR LIBRARIES

40, William IV St., London, W.C.2.

or telephone TEMple Bar 2011

was the model for his Ministry of Truth in *Nineteen Eighty-Four* (1949).[3]

Fougasse's personal work record book reveals all the departments and Ministries he worked for, and how many illustrations, designs, diagrams, posters and press adverts he created. For the Admiralty he produced 17 handbooks and instruction guides including a 'Coxswains Guide', 'Handbook for Smallcraft', 'Eyeshooting Pocketbook' (RN & Merchant Service), 'Naval Pay & Cash Handbook' and literature on Food Waste, as well as posters and designs to encourage people to donate books for the Royal Navy War Libraries.

His war work included designs to promote the Army as a career; to encourage people to join the Auxiliary Territorial Service (ATS); a booklet for the War Office called 'Hide & Seek', a humorous examination of camouflage; illustrations for a 'Rocket Booklet' and guides on 'Light AA Equipment', 'Camouflage', 'Tanks' and the 'Armoured Car Mark I', the 'Light Tank AA Mark I & II', 'Gas Warnings' and 'Daily Physical Charts' (keeping the British healthy through exercise); also literature for the 'Paratroops'. For the Ministry of War Transport his concern was for Road Safety; for the Air Force it was 'Flying Training' and for the Air Ministry he created, among other things, 'Map Notes'. He was tasked to use his design talents to 'speed up production' for the Ministry of Aircraft Production.

Designs were donated to the British Red Cross, notably for the campaign 'National Postal Auctions'. He created a booklet on the conservation of light for the Institute of

Illuminating Engineers. For the Women's Land Army he highlighted the importance of the 'Land Battle', and contributed artwork for the Young Women's Christian Association (YWCA), the Women's Voluntary Service (WVS), the National Association of Training Corps for Girls and the Personal Service League.

Fougasse designed posters for the Soldiers', Sailors' and Airmen's Families Association, (SSAFA) in which he humorously promoted the advice and support, including financial affairs and housing, offered by this organisation. For the Ministry of Supply his ingenuity was harnessed for ideas on 'Saving Time', 'Salvage', 'Waste Collection' and 'Care in Factories'. He worked for the Ministry of Food, to discourage 'Food Waste' and encourage 'Dining Care', as well as the Ministry of Fuel & Power, Ministry of Health, and Ministry of Production. Some of his more memorable images were produced for the Kensington War Savings Fund (Fougasse lived in Kensington). He created vivid and lively posters for the 'Spitfire Fund', 'Salute the Soldier', 'Warship Week', 'War Weapons Week', 'Wings for Victory' and 'War Savings' (General). He transformed Winston Churchill into a determined cigar-smoking tank in 'Salute Our Soldier'.

But Fougasse is best remembered for his 'Careless Talk' posters, published in February 1940. He recorded the posters in his work book under the section entitled 'For the War Effort 1939–1944':

'Careless Talk'   – series of 8 posters
'Careless Talk' for Ships   – 1 poster
'Careless Talk' for U.S. Forces   – 1 poster

The 'Careless Talk' posters for 'Ships' and for 'U.S. Forces' bear the respective strap-lines 'Letters sometimes go astray: <u>Please</u> be careful what you say! <u>Never</u> Mention <u>Ships</u>'; and '<u>Heavens</u>, no – I wouldn't tell a soul!'. They show Adolf Hitler peering from behind a red pillar box; and transformed into a dog in a park with a raised ear to catch the details of a conversation between an American serviceman and a lady. But it was the initial series of eight 'Careless Talk' posters that were the most effective, and are eagerly sought after today by poster collectors. This series shows Hitler, Hermann Goering (Hitler's second-in-command and head of the *Luftwaffe*) and other Nazis 'materializing in the unlikeliest places' listening to indiscreet conversations. Hitler was depicted on a bus and train, by a phone box and hiding within a portrait painting in a gentlemen's club.

Another poster from the series portrays two ladies in a tea room chatting while multiple faces of Hitler formed in the abstract pattern of the wallpaper peer down at them. The image carries the strap-line 'Don't forget that walls have ears!' in Fougasse's

SALUTE
OUR
SOLDIER

"Salute the Soldier" Week in the
Prime Minister's Constituency,
June 10–17.

distinctive handwriting. This was an integral part of almost all his poster designs. When an advertising company insisted on using typefaces instead of Fougasse's handwriting these tended to detract from, rather than harmonise with, the pictorial elements, and the promotional power of the poster was less successful.

Although Fougasse did not number or prioritise the posters, they were arranged by him in the order shown below in ...*and the Gatepost*, a booklet published by the Ministry of Information in 1940. This publication also included Fougasse's text for a BBC radio broadcast on the subject of his poster designs, entitled 'Strictly Between These Four Walls'. The proceeds from the booklet were donated to the Westminster Depot of the British Red Cross Society and St John Hospital Library.

1 'You never know <u>who's</u> listening!'
2 'Of course there's no harm in <u>your</u> knowing!'
3 '...but for Heaven's sake don't say <u>I</u> told you!'
4 'Be careful what you say & where you say it!'
5 'Strictly between you & me...'
6 '...strictly between these four walls!'
7 'Don't forget that walls have ears!'
8 '...but of course it <u>mustn't</u> go <u>any</u> further!'

This series confirmed his status as a leading British propaganda poster designer of the twentieth century. Such is their importance that the V&A acquired preliminary drawings of the posters in 2006. To throw light on their importance it is necessary to examine the background and context of their creation and why Fougasse was confident that they would be successful in relation to competing posters.

During the 1930s and 1940s posters were the most effective means to convey public information on a mass scale. Radio broadcasts were useful but the sets were expensive and individual ownership was very low. Press advertising reached those who bought newspapers and magazines and were able to read. The advantage of posters was that they were free to look at, could be placed in areas that were difficult for people to ignore, and no significant degree of literacy was required to understand the message(s).

The 'Careless Talk Costs Lives' series was conceived at the outset of the War as Home Front propaganda. Wartime Cabinet Minutes of November 1939 reveal that Winston Churchill, then First Lord of the Admiralty, had charged the Cabinet Committee with examining the 'Issue of Warnings Against Discussion of Confidential Matters in Public Places'. Churchill sent a telegram to civil servants and military commanders, urging them to 'check and rebuke expressions of loose and ill-digested opinion in their circle, or by subordinates' and to report and remove without hesitation any of the latter who were

You never know who's listening!

CARELESS TALK
COSTS LIVES

"Of course there's no harm in your knowing!"

CARELESS TALK
COSTS LIVES

"........ but for Heaven's sake don't say **I** told you!"

CARELESS TALK COSTS LIVES

Be careful
what you say
+ where you
say it!

CARELESS TALK
COSTS LIVES

Fougasse
"Strictly between you & me...."
CARELESS TALK COSTS LIVES

"…. *strictly between these four walls !*"

CARELESS TALK COSTS LIVES

Don't forget that walls have ears!

CARELESS TALK COSTS LIVES

Letters sometimes go astray:
Please be careful what you say!

NEVER MENTION SHIPS

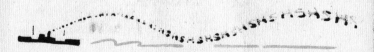

Issued by the British Ship Adoption Society

"Heavens, no—I wouldn't tell a soul!"

CARELESS TALK
COSTS LIVES

SPECIALLY DRAWN AND PRINTED FOR THE AMERICAN RED CROSS IN GREAT BRITAIN

found 'to be consciously exercising a disturbing or depressing influence…'. There were two related worries prompting official concern about wagging tongues. One was danger to security – giving away the position of power stations, the location of munitions plants, factories and airbases, the movements and destinations of ships and troops; and the other was morale.[4]

The Committee Minutes also reveal that the Admiralty, War Office and Ministry of Supply were paying special attention to the need for caution in the use of the telephone, and to 'have affixed notices to their instruments [phones], both at home and in the Field'. Similar steps were being taken by the Air Ministry. Fougasse created books of stamps with a portrait head of Hitler holding a telephone receiver, accompanied by an anti-gossip warning. They were designed to be stuck onto domestic telephones to remind you in Fougasse's words, 'Maybe he's listening too – Careless Talk Costs Lives'. Fougasse featured an illustration of how to affix the stamp, including an example of the stamp itself, in his publication …*and the Gatepost*.

Spy fiction in Britain had steadily grown in popularity from its inception in the 1880s. One of the most popular authors was William Le Queux. His best-known works are the anti-German invasion fantasies *The Great War in England in 1897* (1894) and *The Invasion of 1910* (1906), the latter of which was a phenomenal bestseller. Another hugely popular spy-adventure story was John Buchan's *The Thirty-Nine Steps* (1915), the first of five novels featuring the all-action hero Richard Hannay. Alfred Hitchcock turned it into a film in 1935. Churchill was obsessed with spies and no doubt this reinforced his commitment to stop vital information leaking out through careless talk. Posters were specifically designed to influence

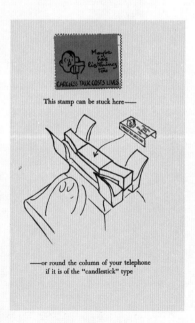

This stamp can be stuck here——

——or round the column of your telephone if it is of the "candlestick" type

the millions performing essential work on the
Home Front. It is impossible to establish just how
many foreign spies were operating in Britain, but
records reveal that during the first 48 hours of the
War about 35 key agents and 400 sub-agents (those
acting for an agent) were apprehended.[5]

The establishment of the Security Service (Secret
Service) coincided with the vogue of spy novels
during the Edwardian era, although British anti-gossip and rumour poster propaganda is
unique to World War II. At the outbreak of World War I Britain had been taken by surprise
and was ill prepared in terms of personnel. The poster propaganda campaigns of that
conflict were preoccupied with recruitment, rather than measures to counter rumour and
gossip. *The Star* newspaper announced on 10 February 1940, when the Fougasse poster
campaign was launched, 'Watch your step for Spies! And they will not be wearing false
wigs or using secret rays'.[6]

Britain was competing with what was then the world's most powerful propaganda
machine. The military historian Peter Darman succinctly summed up the sinister
competition in his publication *Posters of World War II: Allied and Axis Propaganda 1939–
1945*: 'Hitler and the Nazis made great use of propaganda especially posters…The symbols
of the party – the swastika, the eagle, and a wealth of laurel leaves – were seen on posters,
along with strong colours, usually red, black and white. The Nazis turned propaganda into
a religion, and like all religions it needed a high priest. In 1926 they found one when Dr.
Joseph Goebbels was appointed governor of Berlin, and in the 1930s he was appointed
propaganda minister'.

On 13 November 1939 the War Cabinet Minutes recommended a special sub-
committee with representatives of all relevant departments and armed forces chaired by
Mr W. S. Douglas.[7] It was agreed that this sub-committee should have responsibility to
ensure that notices, including posters, retained their effectiveness through repetition and
variety, the latter to avoid boredom. Fougasse's anti-rumour posters
were not the first to be produced but they were the most popular and
were reprinted throughout the war.

The Official Secrets Act (23 November 1939) and Regulation 3 of
the Defence Regulations were not deemed sufficient as a deterrent
against rumour-mongers and gossips and the first full anti-gossip
poster drive was prepared by the Ministry of Information in
December 1939,[8] and the campaign was launched officially (at least to
the media) on 1 February 1940. It was noted in the Cabinet Minutes
that 'An excellent press resulted and copies of the posters [including

the Fougasse series] were reprinted in practically every national daily paper, in many of the provincials, and in two American papers'. They later appeared in the French newspaper *Paris-Soir* (14 February 1940). At that time *Paris-Soir* boasted the largest circulation of any newspaper in Europe – two and a half million copies daily.

Shortly after the start of the War a small-scale letter poster, 'Don't Help the Enemy! Careless Talk May Give Away Vital Secrets' (September 1939, MOI) was approved by the War Office, ready to be put into production immediately. A wide variety of posters, of various sizes, pictorial as well as letter designs, were prepared.[9] Another early letter poster, that resembled a death notice, was captioned, 'Warning. Thousands of lives were lost in the last war because valuable information was given away to the enemy through careless talk. Be On Your Guard' (December 1939, MOI). The War Cabinet Minutes of 13 November 1939 indicate that the General Post Office had responsibility for placing this poster in all telephone kiosks in all town areas throughout the country.

Like 'Don't Help the Enemy' the 'Warning' poster featured a crown device positioned above bold text. The association was that it was King George VI himself exhorting you to pay attention and take the appropriate action. The designers of these posters are not recorded but they have a committee feel, and certainly it is known that one of a similar design concept captioned 'Your Courage, Your Cheerfulness, Your Resolution, Will Bring Us Victory' was largely created by a career civil servant and designed to counter-attack what Duff Cooper (Director, MOI 1940–41) described as 'the talk that is depressing'.[10] This campaign backfired as the message was ambivalent implying that the general population would be making sacrifices for 'Us', which was interpreted as the privileged few.

The crown device also featured in the poster 'Keep Calm and Carry On'. Although this poster, which was a part of a series of letter-posters designed to boost morale and calm nerves after a massive German air bombardment envisaged at the outbreak of the war, was printed, it was never publicly posted. There is no evidence as to why it was not used, but it has been suggested by Bex Lewis, a specialist in propaganda posters, that the poor reception and unpopularity (confirmed by Mass Observation, see later) of the related letter-posters, which were perceived as being patronising and condescending, was a major factor. Around a million posters were printed although very few originals have survived.

A letter written to Fougasse reveals that from the start the MOI was enthusiastic about his voluntary participation. Edwin Joseph Embleton (1907–2000) wrote to him on 3 November 1939: 'Dear Fougasse, I felt I would like to thank you for your kindness in offering to design some anti-rumour posters for us at such short notice'.[11]

Embleton was given a free hand to commission designs from whomever he chose. Posters were commissioned from influential graphic designer Abram Games who was appointed Official War Poster Artist and the only one to hold this position. His assistant

DON'T HELP THE ENEMY!

CARELESS TALK
MAY GIVE AWAY
VITAL SECRETS

WARNING

Thousands of lives
were lost in the last
war because valuable
information was given
away to the enemy
through careless
talk

BE ON
YOUR GUARD

A.0.2   Printed for H.M. Stationery Office by Greycaine Ltd., Watford and London. 7.51- 8666.

was the designer Frank Newbould (1887–1951), who produced propaganda posters, including four for the 'Your Britain, Fight For It Now' campaign. Games fervently believed that 'the biggest impact came from the simplest designs'. He also designed anti-gossip posters. Although Embleton was trained as a commercial and graphic designer he has yet to be personally identified with any wartime posters. He developed the GPD into a 'sort of first class advertising agency selling freedom and victory'. When he set up the department he had a staff of 3 and in 1945 it had risen to over 50. His department comprised 'designers, visualisers, retouchers, letterers and calligraphers, typographers, cartographers and a cartoonist'. Churchill appreciated his contribution and he was later awarded the MBE for his service to the war effort.[12]

Embleton was in his late eighties when he completed an interview for the Imperial War Museum in 1995. What he said and how he sounds (his intonation) reveal a confident, direct, no-nonsense type of gentleman. No doubt he was an effective manager. Dr Paul Rennie from Central Saint Martins College of Art and Design met him towards the end of his life and recalled that 'Edwin was great. He was pretty active and as bright as a button and could remember all sorts. His take on design was very different from, say Abram Games or Tom Eckersley's. He liked the posters with machines in them and he had a lovely old sports car'.

The Cabinet Minutes of 13 March 1940 reveal that by at least this stage of the War Fougasse's designs were by far the most popular pictorial posters and in huge demand. By that date '2,250,100 posters, varying in size from 6¾" x 5¾" to 60" x 40"', had been printed. The most important numerically are the "Official Warning" (1,242,500) and the Fougasse series (734,200). A reprint order has been placed for 453,500, including 248,000 of the latter'. In addition it was recorded that 'Over 1,500,000 have already been posted on voluntary sites. Requests are coming in daily, particularly for the Fougasse series', and that 'The production of new posters is under consideration, but the present designs are so much in demand that it may not be necessary to incur more expenditure yet'.[13]

Embleton thought very highly of the Fougasse series stating in his IWM interview that they 'took the country by storm'. He went on to say that Fougasse had a '…wonderful gift of getting across a message to the Great British public by humour and that priceless gift of appealing to every man and woman personally'.

Many more poster designers would be engaged for the 'Careless Talk' campaign, produced in diverse styles, ranging from the traditional to ultra-modern, but none would approach the enduring mass-popularity of the Fougasse series.

Costs were a major government concern and the 'Careless Talk' campaign depended predominantly on free poster sites and the goodwill of people prepared to display the images without charge. Fougasse was an intellectual artist/designer who fully understood that posters had to be specially designed to satisfy this selfless public gesture. They had to

" Didn't you hear the warning ? "
" Yes, thanks—but we can see quite well enough from here."

be inoffensive and engaging. If you were asking a café owner to hang examples they had to be appropriate for a family audience.

A press conference held at Senate House on 6 February 1940 revealed the enormity and scale of the task:

> The co-operation of many Government Departments, Authorities and organisations, including the Admiralty, War Office, Air Ministry, Ministry of Home Security, the Post Office, Police, the Railways, Banks, Docks and Harbours and local authorities, Tradesmen's organisations and Clubs has been enlisted in this campaign. Approximately 2,000,000 free sites have already been obtained and special types of posters have been designed, some by eminent artists, to suit the site on which they will be placed.

Scotland and Wales were to have their own distinctive posters, the latter printed in Welsh.

The press statement[14] continued:

There are posters for general display – for display in sea-port towns – and posters specially designed for club and other indoor display.

A warning notice which will be widely exhibited makes the following point:-
'Thousands of lives were lost in the last war because valuable information was given away to the enemy through careless talk.' Another poster emphasises this warning by the picture of a sinking ship with the caption 'A few careless words may end in THIS'. It is interesting that this has been designed by Norman Wilkinson,[15] who did so much work on camouflage to help protect our ships against the submarine in the last war. [This poster was well known in North America, and was included in Ealing Studios anti-gossip film *Dangerous Comment*, directed by John Paddy Carstairs (1940), Imperial War Museum Collections.]

A special poster has been designed for exhibition in munition, aircraft and other factories carrying out Government work and bears the following injunction:-
'You know more than other people. You are in a position of trust. Don't let the fighting forces down.
A few careless words may give something away that will help the enemy and cost us lives.
Above all be careful what you say to strangers and in public.'

All these posters are as serious in nature as the subject with which they are concerned, but our people respond to humour sometimes more than to serious injunctions. For that reason, 'Fougasse' so well known as an illustrator has been asked to help in this campaign by producing a number of Anti-gossip posters in colour.

Post offices and telephone kiosks, Underground railway stations, hotels, public houses and restaurants, factories and A.R.P [Air Raid Precaution] posts, barbers' shops and billiard rooms, clubs and village halls, golf clubs and shops mercantile, marine offices and cross-channel steamers, indeed in every place where men and women meet there will be a poster warning all of the danger of careless talk.

The British Legion will be asked to take a prominent part in the distribution of these posters, especially to British Legion branches, Working Men's Clubs, Y.M.C.A, Cinemas, Theatres and Music Halls. [Founded in 1921 The British Legion received the prefix Royal in 1971. It cares and campaigns for those serving and the ex-Service community. Perhaps best known for its Poppy Appeal.]

A FEW
CARELESS WORDS
MAY END IN THIS—

Many lives were lost in the last war through careless talk
Be on your guard ! Don't discuss movements of ships or troops

Arrangements have also been made to place these posters in trams, buses, and motor-coaches as well as at aerodromes and in commercial aeroplanes.

Sir John Reith [then Head of the MOI] is anxious to enlist the help of all organisations and any who have not been approached will be able to obtain the posters by applying to Room 162, Ministry of Information.

On 7 February 1940 *The Times* reported on the poster campaign in a subtitled section called 'Hush! Hush!'.

The Ministry of Information, long patient under the approach of talking too little [there had been widespread condemnation that the MOI was not providing sufficient information in the early stages of the war], now hits back by telling the rest of the country that it talks too much. A fair rejoinder, and very fairly and favourably set out in the posters of its 'anti-gossip campaign'. If one is to look a fool, one is lucky to fall into the hands of Fougasse, because Fougasse's touch is as delicate as it is deadly, and his victims laugh even while they see themselves as Fougasse sees them. Let no man and no woman, in uniform or in plain clothes, imagine that he or she has no personal claim to the attentions of Fougasse...Let Fougasse teach us that there is a Hitler in every hedge, behind every bar, under every table, and lurking, all ears, by every telephone, ready to snap up any unconsidered trifles of information which the latent spot of indiscretion in the most cautious of us may innocently let fall.

Another means to gauge the popularity and effectiveness of the Fougasse posters is to examine the archive records of Mass Observation (M-O). This social research organisation was founded in 1937 by three young men, Tom Harrisson, Charles Madge and Humphrey Jennings, who recruited a team of observers and a panel of volunteer writers to study the everyday lives of ordinary people in Britain. This original work continued until the early 1950s, and the archive is now in the University of Sussex.

The M-O observers were given anonymity. A 25-year-old female thought the 'careless pictures – with Hitler peeping over telephone booths and out of luggage racks at people' were 'excellent'.[16] The observations offer some useful insights into this and other poster

"'EVERY SHILLING'S
A SHELL!"

KENSINGTON WAR WEAPONS WEEK
May 17th—24th

campaigns but are by their very nature highly subjective and sometimes confusing. Another female observer noted down that one of Fougasse's posters showed a woman inside a phone box, when in fact it is clearly a man.

Of the examples of Fougasse's 'Careless Talk' posters that have survived today in good condition, the majority are of a small scale. A document in the British National Archives, and also information from *Advertiser's Weekly* (21 December 1939) throws light on the three recorded sizes and indicates where they were intended to be located. The most popular size was 8 inches (width) by 12½ inches (height) and they were recommended for display in middle-end and upmarket hotels, restaurants, railway restaurants and clubs, billiard halls and billiard rooms of public houses, golf clubs, public houses, hotels and restaurants, tea shops, department store restaurants, railway buffets and restaurants, theatre and music hall bars (inside), hairdressing establishments. They were also intended for display in whatever suitable manner by the Army, Navy and Air Force.[17] There was also a poster 'Double-Crown' in size (20in. x 30in.). A third poster size was produced measuring 25in. x 40in. that was 'applicable to the complete series of eight Fougasse posters' intended for 'Special Railway Double Royal sites'.[18] Double Royal has been the standard poster size used by the London Underground since 1908, and has been used almost exclusively by railway companies.

There were many larger sites that accommodated Double-Quad posters measuring 40in. x 60in., although the nature of Fougasse's poster designs, which required the viewer to examine them in detail at close proximity (especially to read the smaller strap-line) would render his designs ineffective at that size. It is highly unlikely that any Fougasse posters were produced in the Double-Quad size.

On 2 February 1940 '4 small ones (7in. x 14in.) on cardboard (to hang or stand, like Calendars) were noted by a M-O observer at The Spanish Restaurant in Swallow Street...', off Regent Street in London. It is likely that the observer had guesstimated the poster size.[19]

All of Fougasse's war posters were 'framed' with what became his trademark eye-catching (usually uneven) red-line border, or what has been described as a 'red-ribbon'.[20]

This clever device drew attention to the design, acting as a warning or alert. It drew people in. This worked especially well with the inclusion of 'white space' between the 'red-ribbon' and the actual pictorial subject. He used it for many different poster and illustrational campaigns from the 1930s to the end of his career. When exactly he developed this technique is not known, although there are earlier examples of its use. These include a small number of World War I British recruitment posters and also a German anti-gossip poster 'Der Soldat, der Schwätzt…' (The Soldier who Blabs) dated 1918 (a copy of which is in the Imperial War Museum). In each case the width of the red line is regular and is not comparable to Fougasse's irregular line or 'red-ribbon'. The irregular line is a far more effective device to stimulate the eyes of the viewer and encourages closer examination of the pictorial parts and lettering of the poster. It's not clear if Fougasse was familiar with the earlier posters but it is known that he experimented with a red-border and it featured on one of his invitation cards designed for the 25th Annual Dinner of the King's Engineering Society in 1922.

In 1949, the year Fougasse became the editor of *Punch*, he introduced the red-ribbon border to the front cover design, the first example being released on 6 July. As Helen Walasek of the *Punch* Cartoon Library notes, 'Perhaps he'd been longing to use it [from

when he was appointed Art Editor in 1937] and when he achieved total control [as Editor-in-Chief] out came the red paint!' Today, the international bank HSBC uses a similar eye-catching device for its press and poster advertisements.

Fougasse was well aware that his posters had to stand out, because they were competing with other pictorial images and public information. He had strong views about propaganda posters that he articulated in the publication *A School of Purposes* (1946). He offers a definition of the propaganda poster: 'to cover anything stuck up on a wall with the object of persuading the passer-by for the common good'. It identifies three main obstacles that need to be overcome before the poster can succeed. They are:

Firstly, a general aversion to reading any notice of any sort:
Secondly, a general disinclination to believe that any notice, even if read, can possibly be addressed to oneself;
Thirdly, a general unwillingness, even so, to remember the message long enough to do anything about it.

In consequence, the propaganda-poster has obviously three main functions to fulfill:-

(A) It must attract the attention of the passer-by;
(B) It must then persuade him; and
(C) It must keep him persuaded long enough to take action on it.

He noted that too often posters are not tested alongside 'gaudy competitors' in 'natural conditions' but rather in the 'quiet and comfortable sponsors' office'.

Fougasse's suggestion for A was that 'the design should be such as to isolate it from its surroundings: it should always be well barricaded in all round'. Hence, his creation of the red-ribbon border. Secondly,

...still with the object of attracting – and intriguing – the attention of the passer-by, the general visual message should be a judicious mixture of the obvious and the unobvious; say, generally, 90 per cent of the former and 10 per cent of the latter. In other words, the passer-by should always be able to see at a glance what it is about, but not *all* it is about; nine-tenths should catch his eye, and the remaining one-tenth should arouse his curiosity, so that not only is his primary attention caught, and held, but his secondary attention is called into play too. The second suggestion, therefore, is that nine-tenths of the poster should be sufficiently obvious – and interesting – at a distance (both physical and mental) to induce the passer-by to approach near enough both physically and mentally to discover the remaining one-tenth.

He also suggested that a poster design should be tested to see 'how easily it can be defaced by small boys from 5 to 50. (A very slight addition with an irreverent pencil is often sufficient to play havoc with the most inspired design.)'

Under B Fougasse claimed that 'A poster cannot prove anything...the most it can do is to bring to your notice the desirability of a certain course of action'. The object of propaganda, he suggests, is to effect a change of behaviour in the viewer.

Under C, in order to succeed the poster must leave a space for the reader to infer the consequence of not acting in the way suggested. Accordingly, it is important not to attempt to effect too great a change and not to ask too much of the viewer. Lastly, it is crucial to include the viewer in the process so as to make them party to their own persuasion.[21]

Fougasse refused to portray people in a realistic manner. Instead he drew what he called 'formula figures', his trademark linear rag dolls, because he believed that if they did not have specific features everyone could identify with them. As a well-known cartoonist and comic illustrator it is perhaps not surprising that Fougasse favoured humour for communication of public information, believing it more effective than realistic horror images.[22]

Humour, he stressed, 'aims at opening your mind, and the better the quality of humour the wider it opens it'. He believed that 'horror shuts your mind in self-defence and the more efficient the horror content the tighter and quicker it shuts'.

American anti-gossip and rumour propaganda posters adopted both humorous and horror images. Some of the most effective and enduring adopted the latter style to hammer the message(s) home. Some of the best examples were created by Frederick O. Siebel (1886–1968), 'Someone Talked!' (1942) showing a sailor drowning; Anton Otto Fischer (1882–1962), 'A Careless Word...A Needless Loss' (1944), depicting a dead sailor washed up on a beach; and Herbert Morton Stoops' (1888–1948), 'Careless Talk Got There First', showing a dead paratrooper.

" England expects . . . "

Advertiser's Weekly, 8 April 1943, announced that 'American artists from 43 States have gone to war armed with paint-brushes, cameras, paper and a terrific determination to arouse the nation'. An exhibition of their work was held at the Museum of Modern Art in New York where 'visitors have been studying posters urging them to buy War Bonds and to look out for the enemy. This national competition resulted in 2,224 posters submitted and a selection was made of 200... some to be distributed throughout the United States, and three for national distribution to factories and public buildings'.[23]

Designers of British posters were allowed to be more hard-hitting in their designs for active and front-line servicemen in comparison to those serving on the Home Front, but were discouraged from portraying dead British or Allied servicemen, although Abram Games produced an intriguing example 'Your Talk May Kill Your Comrades' (May 1942). This showed careless talk transformed into a spiral-shaped sword skewering three silhouetted servicemen. This was an exception to this general rule. Perhaps it was felt by the censorship official, as James Aulich argues in his publication *War Posters: Weapons of Mass Communication* (2007), that the horror element was toned down or 'neutralized by an abstract style'. American posters also featured images of Italian and Japanese enemy leaders, whereas British posters mainly focused on the threat from Nazi Germany, and therefore favoured images associated with that country. American posters adapted the caption 'Careless Talk' with varying degrees of success. They include Stevan Dohanos's (1907–1994) 'Bits of Careless Talk Are Pieced Together by the Enemy' (1943).

American and Canadian posters also used the entire British slogan 'Careless Talk Costs Lives', and variants on it, some more eye-catching and memorable than others. These included: 'A Careless Word, A Needless Loss', 'A Careless Word Another Cross', 'Closed for the Duration, Careless Talk Can Cost Lives', 'Wanted for Murder, Her Careless Talk Costs Lives', also 'Less Dangerous Than Careless Talk' (the poster depicted a snake), 'Button Your Lip, Loose Talk Can Cost Lives', 'Don't Kill Her Daddy With Careless Talk' (a girl holds a photographic portrait of her father), 'Somebody Blabbed, Button Your Lip', 'Protect His Future...Watch Your Tongue' (which portrayed a small boy), and 'Don't be a Sucker, Keep Your Mouth Shut' that featured a goldfish. Sometimes the posters were a little disjointed in their design (too many visual and word pieces to produce a coherent and unified design) and thus the power of the core message was greatly diminished.

One final argument – and a very simple common-sense one – in favour of the humorous approach was noted by Fougasse:

The propaganda-poster has to get its message across to as many people as it can; however good it is, it can't if it isn't seen. It has therefore got to be displayed as widely as possible. Now, in a totalitarian state this is presumably easy – a 'directive' is issued that the poster is to be displayed everywhere, and displayed it is: in comparatively free democracies, however, this is neither practicable nor desirable. For wide distribution and display, therefore, the success of a propaganda-poster is dependent on the goodwill of people in general – on the readiness for instance of factory-managers, hotel-managers, shop-keepers, etc., to stick it up in their establishments. Now it is obviously not wise to ask the owners of tea-shops, restaurants or public houses to put up horror-propaganda for their clients' comfort, nor is it much use to ask shopkeepers to entertain their customers with gruesome pictorial warnings – if given the choice between realistic and humorous, they will naturally almost invariably choose the humorous, and if given a selection of both (which is usually the case), it is the humorous that they will always actually display.

Not everyone was in agreement with Fougasse's lengthy argument. There were a small number of detractors including Mr T. G. Gibbons who believed that the war was a serious subject. His notice was published in *Advertiser's Weekly* on 21 March 1940: 'There is nothing very comic, however, in a ship being sunk by enemy action as the result of confidential information being spread about by those who imagine that they gain some social prestige by so doing. The loss of human life and vital supplies in wartime can best be illustrated by war pictures showing the devastating results of careless talk'.

Debate has raged over whether Fougasse actually devised the legendary caption 'Careless Talk Costs Lives'. The preliminary poster designs acquired by the V&A reveal that an earlier caption was proposed but not used.[24] It is easy to see why, as 'Careless Talk May Cost Us All Dear' is rather limp by comparison. David Langdon (b.1914), a contemporary of Fougasse and also a fellow propaganda poster designer who devised the memorable cartoon series 'Billy Brown of London Town', believes that Fougasse would have been instrumental in the wording. Langdon thinks it is difficult for people to understand the wide range of skills that were required to be a cartoonist in his day. You had to be an artist, designer, wordsmith, copywriter and salesman.[25] However, bearing in mind the specialist in-house staff that Embleton could call upon it is more

" England expects . . . "

a careless word...

A NEEDLESS LOSS

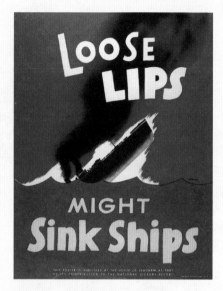

LOOSE LIPS MIGHT Sink Ships

likely that various GPD workers and government ministers would have had some input. The process of determining the captions and originating designs was likely to be more organised and disciplined compared to that of the arbitrary nature of the '*Punch* Table'.

Before its demise, senior *Punch* staff and invited guests attended lunches and dinners around a large Victorian table. 'From its inception circa 1855, it quickly became the custom to discuss the contents of the week's main political cartoon when the meal was over. As the brandy was passed around and the cigars were lit up, the editor would call "Gentlemen, the cartoon!" One of the writers would then suggest what a wheeze it would be to draw Disraeli in the style of a sphinx, or Gladstone the lion fighting the Russian bear, and the unfortunate artist would have to do the best job he could'.[26] The table, carved with the initials of the attendees, is now in the British Library.

The MOI produced numerous variants of the anti-rumour/anti-gossip poster campaigns with varying degrees of success. One of the early letter designs 'Keep It Dark' (issued November 1939) was popular according to studies by M-O. It was a witty play on the need to black out windows in an attempt to protect buildings during the air raids, with the size of the lettering of the slogan getting progressively larger to draw attention to the message. 'If you've news of our munitions KEEP IT DARK, Ships or 'planes or troop positions, KEEP IT DARK, Lives are lost through conversation, Here's a tip for the duration, When you've private information, KEEP IT DARK!' The design had been pre-tested on licensed premises and one M-O observer thought it a 'nice little rhyme'.[27] It also featured in a British anti-gossip film.

The least successful campaign attempted to counter-attack an imagined 'Fifth Column' with a 'Silent Column'. The Spanish Civil War (1936–1939) had given rise to the expression 'fifth column': 'a subversive group that supports the enemy and engages in espionage or sabotage; an enemy in your midst'. The Home Front posters showed 'photographs of typical but dangerous British citizens' who were told to 'Join Britain's Silent Column – the great body of sensible men and women who have pledged themselves not to talk rumour and gossip and to stop others doing it'. The campaign was perceived to be an infringement of civil liberties and the prosecutions of people found guilty for 'defeatist talk' were considered 'sinister'.

Another largely unsuccessful photographic poster campaign was 'They Talked...This Happened' (1940). This series of posters showed ordinary looking citizens, any of who might be a spy. However, the messages were not always clear. For instance in one poster issued in November 1940 the words spoken by an airman's father, 'Cheerio, old lad, good luck tomorrow', were felt to be not sufficiently specific 'to lead to a shot-down plane pictured on the lower half of the poster'.[28]

Later campaigns featured posters aimed at the Home Front, individual and collective depictions of the fighting forces, with the following slogans and strap-lines: 'Never mention sailing dates, cargoes or destinations to anybody, Save Lives, Save Ships, Save Cargoes', 'The more you keep information under your hat – the safer he'll be under his!', as well as, 'Mr Hitler wants to know! He wants to know the unit's name, Where it's going – whence it came, Ships, guns and shells all make him curious, But silence makes him simply Fuehrious'; also 'Zip It'.

One of the most controversial campaigns perceived, by some Members of Parliament – notably Baroness Edith Clara Summerskill, a British physician, feminist, Labour politician and writer – to be sexist is the last named of this 'Careless Talk' group: 'You Forget – But She Remembers', 'Be Like Dad Keep Mum!', 'Tell Nobody – not even Her', and 'Keep Mum She's Not So Dumb!'. This provocative poster was designed by Harold Forster, the artist 'who created *Black Magic*'s (chocolates) alluring ladies', and reminded servicemen to be on their guard when in the company of a beautiful woman who might pass on gossip. *Advertiser's Weekly* (29 May 1941) believed the poster showed 'Olga, the beautiful Spy'. In fact the MOI realised that men were just as likely to gossip as women and their posters were mainly designed to have cross-gender appeal.

In addition to national and provincial pamphlets, posters and press adverts the MOI used other forms of media to combat rumour and gossip. It was noted in the Cabinet Minutes on 13 March 1940 that 'Three ten-minute Anti-Gossip Films are in course of production at the Ealing Studios and will be released at fortnightly intervals, beginning about 22nd March. They will be distributed by Metro-Goldwyn-Mayer by agreement with the trade, and each film is expected to cover at least 2,000 cinemas'.[29] There were also talks given by the BBC, and the subjects featured in conferences and revues. Prominent public speakers were asked to mention the Anti-Gossip Campaign wherever possible and acclaimed writers such as Agatha Christie, E. M. Delafield and W. Somerset Maugham were asked to supply articles or stories on the consequences of careless talk.

The slogan 'Careless Talk Costs Lives', initially not thought to be sufficiently closely connected to the war effort, likely to be revised or superseded, outlived any other.[30] It was parodied in a period poster 'Careless Ropemaking Costs Lives' (1944), and also in modern designs created by contemporary cartoonists such as Nicholas Garland's (b.1935) 'Careless Talk Costs Political Lives', published in *The Daily Telegraph*, 13 February 1995. It is an adaptation of the Fougasse poster 'You never know who's listening!' depicting Margaret Thatcher, Norman Tebbit and Michael Portillo. Also Steve's Bell's (b.1951) 'Careless Pork Costs Lives', with the embedded text 'Don't tell the pig, but between you and me foot and mouth is no worse than a bout of flu! Caution – This is a kill everything that flaps, squawks or crawls area – Apologies to Fougasse', published in *The Guardian*, 9 March 2001.

Millions of 'Careless Talk' posters were produced throughout the war, and they are remembered by many who lived through it. His designs were also printed onto handkerchiefs, ladies' jackets and dresses (V&A collections). In *World Press News*, 8 February 1940, it was reported that Sir Kenneth Clark (Director of the National Gallery, Chairman of the War Artists' Advisory Committee and Head of the MOI Film Unit) 'told a Press conference on Tuesday of this week that anti-gossip posters [the press article featured one of Fougasse's posters] have had a great effect with the B.E.F. [British Expeditionary Forces]'. Anti-gossip posters were produced in Germany and France during World War I. During World War II the largest numbers were produced in Britain, the USA and Canada; they were also produced in Australia, France, Germany, Greece, Japan, New Zealand and Russia. No significant posters appear to have survived from Italy during the Fascist era.

The 'Careless Talk' slogan rather than the campaign, also resonates with those who 'never saw a bomber or heard a siren'.[31] In 1950 it was claimed that the future Queen, Princess Elizabeth, stated: 'How carelessly we should have talked during the war but for Fougasse'.[32]

The more we are together,
the more uncomfortable we'll be.

<u>PLEASE</u> PASS ALONG THE PLATFORM

CHAPTER 4

LONDON UNDERGROUND POSTERS & PUNCH POST WAR

Fougasse started producing designs and posters for the London Underground in the 1920s, but his finest work was realised in the following two decades. One early example, depicting a sectional view of a London street and the tube tunnels below, was praised by the *Morning Advertiser* on 18 April 1925. The caption suggested that above ground there was 'too much waiting and too little room', while below ground there was 'plenty of room and no waiting'.[1]

The differing sizes of Underground posters are discussed in detail in the publication *London Transport Posters: A Century of Art and Design* (2008), jointly edited by David Bownes and Oliver Green. They ranged from small 'Panel Posters' of non-standard sizes used in the 1920s and 30s and placed on glass screens just inside the doors of the carriages, to the standard poster size of 40in. x 25in. (Double Royal). Larger posters were also produced of 40in. x 50in. (Quad Royal) and 60in. x 40in. (Four Sheet or Double Quad). In addition there was also a poster 30in. x 20in. (Double-Crown) for display on the front panels of buses and the side panel of trams.

In the mid 1940s, London Underground commissioned Fougasse to produce his finest transport posters encouraging commuters and travellers to avoid the rush hour, stand

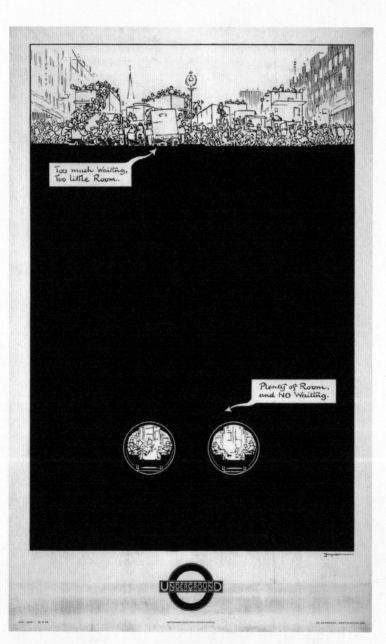

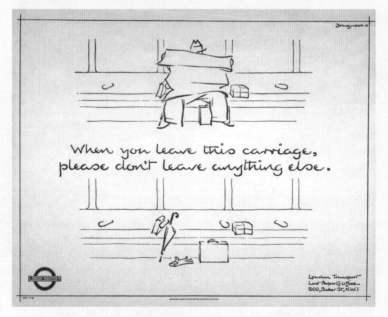

Don't wait till the shop's just closing for the night

DO YOUR SHOPPING EARLY ⊖

on the right of the escalator, have their tickets ready for inspection, beware the penalties of fare evasion, to pass along the platform, give up seats for the elderly, and not leave personal possessions behind.

One man stands out above all others for creating the identity of the London Underground. 'As head of the London Underground in the 1910s and 1920s and of the newly merged London Transport in the 1930s, Frank Pick (1878–1941) was instrumental in establishing the world's most progressive public transport system and an exemplar of design management'. Pick's strategy was to use artistic images to persuade commuters to visit London's attractions during their leisure time.[2] He also commissioned artists and designers to encourage commuters to take notice of the rules, regulations and etiquette of public transport.

'From the red, white and blue roundel that has symbolised the London Underground since the 1910s, Edward Johnston's clear easy to read at a distance typeface in use from 1916 [a variation of his original, named New Johnston, is still used by London Underground today] and the diagrammatic map designed by Harry Beck which enabled 1930s Londoners to find their way around the fast-expanding underground train network, to publicity posters and upholstery fabrics…', Pick could claim credit for their successful implementation.[3]

Unhappy with the poster designs from freelance commercial artists, Pick encouraged submissions from established and emerging artists, who soon considered it prestigious to be invited to work for London Underground. Among the extensive roll call of notable artists commissioned were Charles Pears (1873–1958), Edward Wadsworth (1889–1949), Hans Schleger ('Zero') (1898–1976), the US-born Edward McKnight Kauffer (1890–1954) and surrealist Man Ray (1890–1977), the acclaimed British painter Graham Sutherland (1903–1980), Tom Eckersley OBE (1914–1996) and Abram Games.

In 1940 Frank Pick resigned from London Transport and was appointed, albeit briefly, as director of the MOI a post he 'tackled with characteristic zeal and courage'. He held the post for only a year before his premature death.

Everyone who used public transport and the London Underground in the 1940s saw Fougasse's work. In 1946 the writer and politician Sir Alan Patrick Herbert wrote: 'Surely the whole population knows a "Fougasse" when they see it – and can tell a "Fougasse" across three platforms'.[4] His work record book indicates that he designed seven posters for London Underground and two posters for The London Passenger Transport Board on the subjects of 'Anti-Litter' and 'Lost-Property'. However, this does not square with the official records of London Underground whose database indicates 13 posters and 7 panel posters [presumably the 7 recorded by Fougasse] that were produced between the years 1925 to 1944.[5] Fougasse's work record book was compiled towards the end of his life and it is likely that through a memory lapse he overlooked his earlier work.

Fougasse was still heavily involved in the running of *Punch* and in 1949 he became the seventh magazine editor, the first (and last) to have in effect drawn his way to the post. He reformed the design, layout and typography of the magazine, an example of this being that front-page advertisements were removed. He was responsible for two special issues of *Punch* published to celebrate the centenary of the Festival of Britain (1951) and the Coronation (1953). The former front cover was an impish parody of Abram Games' official Festival logo.[6]

As Hillier accurately asserts, his 'interest was in art and technical matters; he left the choice of writers almost entirely to Humphry Francis Ellis MBE (1907–2000). Ellis gained a double first from Magdalen College, Oxford. He submitted to the magazine in 1931, and became a staff writer two years later. In 1949 Ellis was both the literary and deputy editor, posts that he held until 1953, when he resigned in protest at the appointment of Malcolm Muggeridge as editor. Muggeridge was shocked at what he believed to be the very inward looking, conservative and highly traditional manner in which *Punch* was run. Fougasse had 'restyled the magazine, removing the advertisements from the front cover, and dropped the second cartoon', but he did not give *Punch* an editorial point of view.[7]

The bleak post-war years were made somewhat brighter by Fougasse's patronage of gifted comic artists whose work regularly appeared in the magazine. They included Rowland Emett OBE

PLEASE STAND ON THE RIGHT
OF THE ESCALATOR

"Isn't it lucky I'm not in a hurry?"

<u>PLEASE</u> HAVE YOUR TICKET READY AT THE BARRIER

Incredulity

(1906–1990), best known for designing the Heath Robinson-esque machines for the film *Chitty Chitty Bang Bang* (1968); also Ronald Searle (b.1920), prisoner of war, and perhaps still best remembered as the creator and illustrator of *St. Trinian's,* a fictional girls' boarding school that later became the subject of a popular series of comedy films.[8] The first *St. Trinian's* cartoon appeared in 1941. Fougasse also encouraged Quentin Blake (b.1932) whose first drawings were published in *Punch* while he was 16 and still at school. He continued to draw for *Punch*, *The Spectator* and other magazines over many years, while at the same time entering the world of children's books with *A Drink of Water* by John Yeoman in 1960.[9]

Peter Mellini noted that Fougasse also encouraged several younger up-and-coming cartoonists, 'such as Thomas Derrick, David Langdon, Paul Crum (Roger Pettiward), J. H. Dowd, and Anton (Antonia Yeoman and H. Underwood Thompson)' who 'gravitated to his simplified line and compressed jokes', and that he 'nurtured such unique talents as Pont (Graham Laidler)'.

After Fougasse's retirement from the staff of *Punch* he continued to contribute to the publication. He designed hundreds of posters, and illustrated more than 30 books and pamphlets. He was a member of the BBC's *The Brains Trust*, a popular informational radio and later television programme during the 1940s and 1950s. The chairman was his friend and literary collaborator William Donald Hamilton McCullough (1901–1978), who was a British writer and broadcaster. He was the first question-master of *The Brains Trust* radio programme from its foundation in 1941.

Fougasse was a particularly charming and amusing man and after an hour or so of his company you would have laughed so much you almost felt you had been amusing too. He

ALL THE SAME, YOU KNOW, THOSE AEROPLANES THAT FLY OVER TWICKENHAM MUST GET RATHER A JOLLY VIEW
OF THE GAME.

OUR PREDECESSORS' GAMES

I DARESAY OUR PREDECESSORS GOT A CERTAIN AMOUNT OF PLEASURE OUT OF THEIR GAMES, BUT—

IT SEEMS HARD TO BELIEVE— THAT—

THEY— EVER—

ACTUALLY— WON ANY.

was much in demand as an after-dinner speaker. He belonged to a number of clubs and societies – Athenaeum, Arts, Beefsteak, Garrick, Hurlingham, Omar Khayyam (twice President), a Fellow of the Zoological Society, Member of the Society for the Study of Animal Behaviour, Member of the Lochaber and Skye Gatherings. But according to Tom Bird, the artist's nephew, 'he didn't visit the clubs much and he wasn't really clubbable, and of course as he was a Christian Scientist he didn't drink or smoke'. To some perhaps he was perceived as a little prudish, at least in terms of his personal life, but this did not detract from his delicious sense of humorous nonsense.

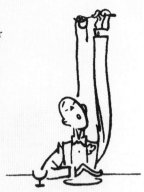

Christian Science was very much part of both Mollie's and Fougasse's lives. In 1933 they both became Christian Scientists. Founded by Mary Baker Eddy in 1866, Christian Science was a spiritual practical solution to health and moral issues. Fougasse's beliefs, and those of his wife, related directly to the fact that they had both experienced bad health and, especially for Fougasse, survived a near-death experience in Gallipoli. He believed his survival was a miracle due to his faith. Among other things he taught, or at any rate held, Christian Science sessions at Eton College for sons with Christian Science parents during the period 1953–55. He served on the Lecture Committee of the Church (1937–39), was a Board Member (1955–57) and Chairman in 1956. The couple attended the church in Curzon Street.

Fougasse was extraordinarily knowledgeable on a wide range of subjects. He would do *The Times* crossword while sitting on the lavatory after breakfast – all except one clue, which he left for Mollie to fill in during the day. In a marriage of 50 years she very seldom managed to do so. Fougasse died of cancer of the testicles in great pain on 11 June 1965.[10] In the year after his death an exhibition of his work was held at the Fine Art Society in London.

David Langdon first contributed for *Punch* in 1937. Now in his nineties he vividly remembers Fougasse as a kind, quiet, modest man, and when he did speak up at meetings, everyone would listen intently. There were no sides to him. He created humour that had a universal appeal. Although he was unashamedly middle class, his was a sense of humour that could be enjoyed by everyone, adult and adolescent alike; there was, and this remains true to this day, nothing in his work to offend anyone. Interestingly an early assessment on Fougasse's 'lightly drawn and brightly coloured' posters by M-O, reported in *Advertiser's Weekly* on 29 February 1940, reveals that 'early reactions suggest their appeal to be (a) slightly sophisticated, (b) somewhat middle class'. One shows clubmen in huge armchairs, another diners-out with shaded lights and white wine. But the new campaign is an obvious advance, in terms of mass appeal on earlier efforts'.

Dr Paul Rennie believes that 'Fougasse is certainly not snobby or political as Bateman or Low [Sir David Low 1891–1963]… He is also too well mannered for the *Private Eye*

"It seems that the one in pink is their wicket-keeper's sister."

generation that came after about 1960'.

Fougasse was a life member of the British Legion; Fellow of the Society of Industrial Artists; Fellow of the Royal Society of Arts; Member of the Council of the Society of Graphic Artists; County Councillor, Monmouthshire; Member of the Central Council, NSPCC; Master of the Art Workers' Guild; Member of Council of the Imperial Arts League; Member of Council of the Royal Albert Hall (Chairman of Catering Committee); and Chairman and Hon. Artist for the Universities Federation for Animal Welfare (UFAW).

In his own work Fougasse pared down human activity with such economy as to suggest the essence of modern life and this approach also had a significant effect on advertising. Hillier summed up his contribution: 'Economy of line and colour, a delightful sense of nonsense and an ability to make others laugh at themselves were among his outstanding qualities'. Some of his finest small-scale cartoons need no captions. Perhaps he is the cartoonist equivalent to Edward Lear's delightful literary nonsense.

He refined his cartooning style into modernist shorthand – what Hillier called 'his hieroglyphic almost notional style'. In his personal survey of modern British and American humorous art, *The Good-Tempered Pencil* (1956), Fougasse wrote, 'pictorial humour is simply a short hand by which humorous ideas may be absorbed by the reader with the minimum of effort'.

He pioneered the idea that humour is more important than art. He believed that it is really better to have a good idea with a bad drawing than a bad idea with a good drawing.

Ruth Walton of the V&A, which holds the national collection of posters – some 18,000 examples – claims that 'his designs were so memorable and influential that they are still

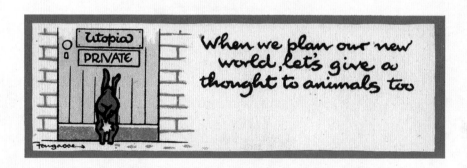

talked about today', and that he is '…arguably the best known and best loved exemplar of British poster art'. Well, the last claim (opinion) should be clarified. It was written in the context of an attempt, a successful one, to secure a grant from the Art Fund to acquire Fougasse's eight preliminary drawings for 'Careless Talk'. It would be more accurate to temper this claim to state that Fougasse is '…arguably the best known and best loved exemplar of British *Home Front* poster art'.

Fougasse was without a doubt one of the most brilliant and endearing cartoonists of the first half of the twentieth century. Hillier observed that, 'As his cartoons relied more on telling observation rather than on exaggeration, his drawings are a vivid pictorial chronicle of "U" [upper and upper-middle-class] Britain between the Great War and the mid-1950s'. But with the changing tastes of post-war Britain, the wider choice of colour magazines with more sophisticated illustrations, the dwindling circulation of *Punch* magazine, and the dawn of the television age his reputation gradually faded. His obituary that appeared in *The Times* on Monday, 14 June 1965 was economical in lines: 'Death – June 11th at 115, Swan Court, SW3, Kenneth Bird, C.B.E. (Fougasse), husband of Mollie. Cremation private. Please, no flowers'.

NOTES

Introduction

1 Bevis Hillier, *Fougasse*, Elm Tree Books, England, 1977

CHAPTER 1

1 Bird Family Records & Reminiscences
2 Bevis Hillier, *Fougasse*, Elm Tree Books, England, 1977
3 Fougasse work book, includes paid and unpaid work, biography, exhibition list etc
4 Bird Family Records & Reminiscences
5 Bird Family Records & Reminiscences
6 Acquisition report for the Fougasse Archives, Victoria & Albert Museum

CHAPTER 2

1 Bevis Hillier, *Fougasse*, Elm Tree Books, England, 1977
2 The earliest example of an 'Episodic' cartoon within the pages of *Punch* was produced by Richard Doyle (1824–1883), who devised the front cover of the magazine, entitled 'Brown, James and Robinson go to the Zoological Gardens', 1850.
3 Naomi Games, *Abram Games: His Life and Work*, New York, 2003
4 Bevis Hillier, *Fougasse*, Elm Tree Books, England, 1977
5 The Mighty Fougasse', *Advertiser's Weekly*, 29 February 1940
6 Percy Venner Bradshaw, *Fougasse of Punch*, Art and Industry, Vol. 46, No. 275, May 1949
7 Bird Family Records & Reminiscences
8 *Punch* Archives & Records
9 Op.cit
10 Bird Family Records & Reminiscences
11 Fougasse work book
12 Peter Mellini, *Fougasse*, DNB
13 Embleton commissioned the prolific painter and etcher Frank Henry Mason (1876–1955) RSMA, RI, to produce the first pictorial poster of the War entitled 'The British Navy guards the freedom of us all' (1939). He was proud of the outcome and personally gave it 'full-marks'. Reference: Imperial War Museum interview (on cassette tape) with Edwin Joseph Embleton, 25 November 1995 (IWM 16340).
14 Bird Family Records
15 Victoria & Albert Museum Fougasse Archives – acquisition report, and also see Peter Mellini, *Fougasse*, DNB
16 Fougasse work book
17 Chris Beetles, 8 & 10 Ryder Street, St. James's, London, SW1Y 6QB

CHAPTER 3

1 PRO INF 1/637
2 Imperial War Museum interview with Edwin Joseph Embleton, 25 November 1995 (IWM ref: 16340).
3 PRO INF 1/86, General Production Division: Staff and Functions, 26 August, 1940
4 PRO CAB/67/2/38. See also Angus Calder *The People's War: Britain, 1939–45*, Jonathan Cape, 1969
5 I. Allinson, *A History of Modern Espionage*, Hodder & Stoughton, 1965
6 Mass Observation (M-O) Archive, University of Sussex
7 PRO CAB/67/2/38
8 Dr Rebecca (Bex) Mary Lewis 'Careless Talk Costs Lives', *Everyone's War* magazine, No.15, 2007
9 '"Anti-Gossip" Drive by M. of I., Series of Double-Crown and Smaller Posters', *Advertiser's Weekly*, 21 December 1939
10 M-O FR 286, 'Prediction, restriction and jurisdiction: Enemy propaganda, control of rumour, restriction of civilian activity and reaction of public to new military-civil courts', July 1940, quoting Duff Cooper (Director MOI, 1940–41)

11 Embleton was born in Hornsey, got a scholarship to Hornsey Art School and became studio manager of Odhams Press. At the age of 32 he was appointed studio manager of the GPD and reported for work on 4 September 1939. (IWM Interview 1995, ref. 16340). See also Bevis Hillier, *Fougasse*, Elm Tree Books, England, 1977.

12 Imperial War Museum interview with Edwin Joseph Embleton, 25 November 1995 (IWM ref. 16340). Also, see Archive of Art & Design (National Art Library, V&A Museum ref. AAD/1996/4)

13 PRO CAB/67/5/29

14 Mass Observation Archive, University of Sussex

15 Norman Wilkinson (1878–1971), like Fougasse, served at Gallipoli. In 1917 he invented 'Dazzle-Camouflage', deciding that, since it was all but impossible to hide a ship on the ocean (if nothing else, the smoke from its smokestacks would give it away), a far more productive question would be: How can a ship be made to be more difficult to aim at from a distance through a periscope? In his own words, he decided that a ship should be painted 'not for low visibility, but in such a way as to break up her form and thus confuse a submarine officer as to the course on which she was heading' [ref. Norman Wilkinson, *A Brush With Life*, Seeley Service, 1969]. He was also a War Artist in World War II and painted marine subjects for the ocean liner *Olympic* and her sister-ship *Titanic*.

16 M-O T/C 43 4-B, (F25B), 'Silent Column overheards', undated but probably mid-1940.

17 PRO INF 2/95 (Parts 1–2)

18 Op.cit

19 Mass Observation Archive, University of Sussex

20 Paul Rennie, 'Fougasse & the Purpose of Wit', *Illustration Magazine*, December 2007

21 Op.cit

22 Op.cit

23 'Telling America Through the Horror Poster', *Advertiser's Weekly*, 8 April 1943

24 The author examined the eight preliminary 'Careless Talk' designs on 26 November 2009. They are crude in execution and differ in various details in relation to the printed poster images. Initial reaction is to question their authenticity, or perhaps they are comparable to the story of the preliminary drawing of 'The Man Who Sneezed' outlined in Chapter 2. Embleton stated categorically in his IWM interview in 1995 that the original 'finished designs' were destroyed during the Blitz.

25 Author's conversations with David Langdon, March 2010

26 Origins of the '*Punch* Table' *Punch* Archives & Records

27 Dr Elizabeth (Bex) Mary Lewis 'Careless Talk Costs Lives', *Everyone's War* magazine, No.15, 2007

28 Op.cit

29 PRO CAB/67/5/29

30 PRO INF/1/250, Sub-Committee on Anti-Gossip chaired by Sir Kenneth Clark, Friday, 14 March 1941. See also Dr Rebecca (Bex) Mary Lewis, *The Planning, Design and Reception of British Home Front Propaganda Posters of the Second World War*, University College Winchester, (unpublished), page 197.

31 Malcolm Smith, *Britain and 1940: History, Myth and Popular Memory*, Routledge, 2000

32 Ernest O. Hauser, quoted in 'The British Think It's Funny', *Saturday Evening Post*, 28 January 1950, p.27

CHAPTER 4

1 Bevis Hillier, *Fougasse*, Elm Tree Books, England, 1977

2 Design Museum, London (www.DesignMuseum.org)

3 Op.cit

4 Fougasse, *A School of Purposes* (1946)

5 Oliver Green, *Underground Art*, Studio, 1990

6 Bevis Hillier, *Fougasse*, Elm Tree Books, England, 1977

7 Peter Mellini, *Fougasse*, DNB

8 Ronald Searle (www.RonaldSearle.com)

9 Quentin Blake (www.QuentinBlake.com)

10 Bird Family Records & Reminiscences

EXHIBITIONS IN PUBLIC & PRIVATE GALLERIES
(source: Fougasse's work record book)

Fine Art Society, Oct 1924
British Empire Exhibition, 1924
British Empire Exhibition, 1925
Gummerson's Gallery Stockholm, 1925
Rugby Football Exhibition, Sporting Gallery, 1925
Boxing Exhibition, Sporting Gallery, 1925
Humour Exhibition, King Edward Hospital, 1925
Fine Art Society, May 1926
Royal Scottish Academy Centenary Exhibition, 1926
Public Art Gallery, Worthing, June 1927
Public Art Gallery, Sunderland, Oct 1928
Public Art Gallery, West Hartlepool, Dec 1928
Fine Art Society, Jan 1929
Sporting Gallery, June 1929
Lincoln Art Gallery, April 1929
Reid & Lefevre, Glasgow, Jan 1930
Bennett's Gallery, Glasgow, Oct 1933
Altrincham Art Gallery, Dec 1934
Society of Graphic Artists (yearly)

ARCHIVES & COLLECTIONS
The Cartoon Museum, London
Imperial War Museum (Duxford and London)
King's College, London, Library and Archive
London Transport Museum
Museum of London
National Archives, Kew
National Army Museum, London
Punch Magazine Archive, London,
Tate Britain, London
Victoria & Albert Museum, London (includes more than 400 items by and associated with Fougasse. These include commercial illustrations, designs, posters, pamphlets, publications, also personal and family artefacts and papers. The collection includes early designs for the series of eight 'Careless Talk Costs Lives' anti-rumour / gossip poster campaign.

FOUGASSE PUBLICATIONS
(source: Fougasse's work record book)

A Gallery of Games (1921)
Drawn at a Venture (1922)
P.T.O. (1926)
E & O.E. (1928)
Aces Made Easy, 1934 (with W. D. H. McCulloch)
Fun Fair (1934)
You Have Been Warned: A Complete Guide to the Road, 1935 (with W. D. H. McCulloch)
The Luck of the Draw, 1936
Drawing the Line Somewhere, 1937
Stop or Go: A Diary for 1939 (1938)
Jotsam, 1939
...and the Gatepost, 1940 (Ministry of Information)
The Changing Face of Britain, 1940
Running Commentary, 1941
The Little Less..., 1941 (with Guy Reed) (Ministry of Information)
Sorry No Rubber, 1942
Just a Few Lines, 1943 (with Arthur Bird, illustrated verses)
Family Group, 1944
Home Circle, 1945
A School of Purposes, 1946
You and Me, 1948
Question Mark, 1949
US, 1951
The Neighbours: an Animal Anthology,1954 (proceeds to UFAW)
The Good Tempered Pencil, 1956
Between the Lines, 1958

SELECTED READING

Jim Aulich, *War Posters: Weapons of Mass Communication*, Thames & Hudson, 2007
Fougasse, *A School of Purposes*, Methuen, 1946
Bevis Hillier, *Fougasse*, Elm Tree Books, 1977
Richard Slocombe, *British Posters of the Second World War*, IWM, 2010
Margaret Timmers (editor), *The Power of the Poster*, V&A Publications, 1999

For an extensive book list visit www.CarelessTalkCostsLives.co.uk

PICTURE CREDITS

Fougasse artworks and cartoons that are not the copyright of *Punch*, or other designated copyright holders, are reproduced by kind permission of Nicky Bird and C.K. Bird's nephew and family. Reproduced with permission of Punch Ltd, www.punch.co.uk 18, 20, 21, 22, 23, 27, 28, 31, 32, 33 (detail), 35, 64, 87, 88; London Transport Museum 78, 80, 81 (both), 82, 83, 84, 85; Imperial War Museum 62 (PST_13942), 66 (PST_13957); The National Archives, Kew 77 (INF3_229); with UFAW's approval (www.ufaw.org.uk) 17 (top), 90 (bottom); the NSPCC's approval (www.nspcc.org.uk) 12; author's collection 61, 74 (both).

The following galleries, organisations and individuals kindly supplied images for the book: Chris Beetles Ltd (www.chrisbeetles.com), Henry Sotheran Limited (www.sotherans.co.uk), Paul and Karen Rennie (www.rennart.co.uk), Austin Reed (www.austinreed.co.uk).

"I always say to them —'well, why do you want to go fast?'"

ABOUT THE AUTHOR

James Taylor MA (Hons) FRSA studied at the Universities of St Andrews and Manchester. Formerly Head of Victorian Paintings at Phillips Fine Art Auctioneers, he was for ten years curator of paintings, drawings and prints, and exhibition organiser at the National Maritime Museum. From 1999 he has been a freelance art consultant, exhibition organiser and author. His publications include *Marine Painting* (Studio Editions, 1995), *Yachts on Canvas* (Conway, 1998) and *The Voyage of the 'Beagle'* (Conway and Naval Institute Press, 2008).